The Vitality
of the Arthurian Legend

The Vitality
of the Arthurian Legend

A Symposium

ODENSE UNIVERSITY PRESS · 1988

The publication of this volume was made possible
by the generous support of the Danish Research Council
for the Humanities and by a grant from Ingeniør Knud Højgaards Foundation.

Proceedings of the Twelfth International Symposium
organized by the
Centre for the Study of Vernacular Literature
in the Middle Ages held at Odense University
on 16-17 November, 1987

Edited by
Mette Pors

© 1988 by Odense University Press
Printed by Mammens Bogtrykkeri A/S
ISBN 87 7492 689 6
Cover by Lizet Baré

Contents

✠

Acknowledgements	7
Introduction	9
A City Built to Music: An Introduction to the Story of Arthur	
By GRAHAM D. CAIE	13
The Historical Origins of the Arthurian Legend	
By GEOFFREY ASHE	25
Medieval French Arthurian Literature: Recent Progress and Critical Trends	
By KEITH BUSBY	45
Middle English Arthurian Romance: The Repetition and Reputation of Gawain	
By PHILLIP C. BOARDMAN	71
Arthur Coming Alive Again: 18th-Century Medievalism and the Beginnings of a Modern Myth	
By KURT GAMERSCHLAG	91
My Search for Morgaine Le Fay	
By MARION ZIMMER BRADLEY	105
The Knight Errant: The Quest for Integrity	
By RICHARD CAVENDISH	111
Members and Associate Members of the Symposium	123
Medieval Menu of the Banquet	125

Acknowledgements

✠

The symposium on The Vitality of the Arthurian Legend took place at Odense University on the 16th and 17th of November, 1987, and was the 12th in a series of annual symposia arranged by the Centre for the Study of Vernacular Literature in the Middle Ages. This book presents the lectures of the symposium in the order they were delivered.

We are grateful to the authors, and to the many guests from Denmark, England, Norway, Finland, and Germany, who all contributed to the interesting discussions and the liveliness of the occasion. As for practicalities we are much indebted to our secretary Connie Beck for her contribution to the smooth running of the symposium and for the transition of the lectures into this book; to Odense University Press for their professional assistance in the publication process; to Lizet Baré for creating the painting adorning the lecture-room and the cover of the present volume; to the Danish press for giving us such generous coverage; and finally to Restaurant Amfita for braving the perils of medieval cooking and thereby helping us make our finishing galla-dinner an event to be remembered!

We also wish to express our gratitude to the Danish Research Council for the Humanities, Ingeniør Knud Højgaard's Foundation, the Carlsberg Foundation, and the Foundation of Queen Margrethe the Second and Prince Henrik of Denmark for their exceedingly generous financial support, which made not only the symposium but also the publication of the proceedings possible.

July 1988   The editor.

Introduction

✠

It was with great joy that I accepted the opportunity of organizing a symposium on King Arthur, which appropriately could be named The Vitality of The Arthurian Legend, because it was precisely that vitality as reflected in its geographical and temporal dissemination we wished to focus on.

Unlike many other stories, legends, and myths, the Matter of Britain possesses a quality, which makes it adaptable to all ages. Every century, and in this century every decade, has made important contributions to the body of Arthurian stories, and yet the kernel remains the same. The story of Alexander the Great was popular for many centuries but lost most of its appeal with the death of the "heroic society" and was, incidentally, ousted by the Arthurian legend, maybe because the former had no room for the courtly love ideal, which became so important to literature and society in 12th-century Europe. The only other story to rival the popularity of the Matter of Britain in European minds is the New Testament, which forms the basis of the Christian religion and is consequently charged with powerful emotions, touching the very foundations of western man's spirit and existence. The stories concerning Jesus Christ are "fixed" in the sense that we have the Bible as almost contemporary proof, but in the case of Arthur we do not as yet know of one specific contemporary document testifying to his royalty, achievements, career, course of life, and vicissitudes of love and warfare. Hence, around the fragile kernel there is ample scope for imagination and conjecture, hopes and dreams to flourish. Never has so much been written based on so many "maybe's". And this is where the adaptability lies.

Dr. Graham Caie from Copenhagen University opened the proceedings with "A City Built to Music", in which he beautifully brings out both the diversity and unity of the Arthurian legend, showing the former by mentioning the variety of arts that celebrate the Matter of Britain, and proving the latter by drawing attention, through numerous well-chosen literary quotations spanning more than 800 years, to the essence of human existence as it is presented in the Arthurian stories.

In "The Historical Origins of the Arthurian Legend" Geoffrey Ashe speculates whether the question "did King Arthur exist?" is the right question to ask, and he convincingly discusses his theory put forward in his "The Discovery of King Arthur" published in 1985. In this book Mr. Ashe is the first scholar to take Geoffrey of Monmouth's statement to the effect that Arthur campaigned on the Continent seriously and consequently found that the historical "Riothamus" and his deeds may in fact constitute the basis for the Matter of Britain. To quote Mr. Ashe: "That in the King of the Britons who went to Gaul we at last have an acceptable starting-point for the legend, a documented origin. After so many years of debate and dispute, that, surely, is progress."

Keith Busby's "Medieval French Literature: Recent Progress and Critical Trends" elucidates the importance of Chretien de Troyes for the Arthurian legend. Chretien was the first to sophisticate the stories of Arthur into the medieval romance that were to inspire not only Europe but also culture outside Europe. Keith Busby furthermore gives a very well-informed view of medieval French Arthurian literature. However, Professor Busby's emphasis is to be found in the many various approaches to Arthurian literature and in estimating the value of the different critical methods in vogue the last thirty years or so.

In view of the fact that medieval French Arthurian literature inspired the English, the natural continuation to Professor Busby's paper was a lecture on the medieval English Arthuriana, delivered by Professor Phillip Boardman. In "Middle English Arthurian Romance: The Repetition and Reputation of Gawain" Professor Boardman convincingly demonstrates how, in the later Middle Ages, the figure of Sir Gawain increasingly came to epitomize the best of the Arthurian knightly ideal, frequently banishing Arthur to the background as the ridiculed cuckold. Sir Gawain comes to represent the person, who does the right thing, not because of fear of public shame but because of private conscience.

Bridging the gap between medieval literature and modern times, Professor Kurt Gamerschlag lectured on "Arthur Coming Alive Again: 18th-Century Medievalism and the Beginnings of a Modern Myth". Readers of this book will notice with interest, how differently the figure of Arthur is used in this century: he is perceived more as a stay-at-home with no imperial aspirations than as the mighty European conqueror the Middle Ages needed to see him as. Professor Gamerschlag also explains the whimsicalities that arose from a mingling of Celtic and Nordic lore, and how influenced the Arthurian legend is in the 18th century by William Shakespeare's dramas. Professor Gamerschlag also draws our attention to why only very few of the literary Arthurian works of this period have remained popular with us in the present age, though temporally closer to us than those of the Middle Ages.

Marion Zimmer Bradley, who published "The Mists of Avalon" in 1982, was invited to speak in her capacity as a fiction-writer and therefore as a representative of modern Arthurian fiction. In her novel, Mrs. Bradley shifts the focus from the King and his knights to Morgaine le Fay, priestess, sorcerer, wise-woman, witch – the woman, who is as powerful as her brother and lover, King Arthur. Throughout "The Mists of Avalon" Mrs. Bradley brilliantly shows the opposition, as it *may* have been, between the ancient Celtic religion with a touch or more of matriarchy, and the Christian religion with its patriarchy. Her novel is a fine example of how the old Arthurian stories can be adapted in the 1980'ies to express views on feminism, attitudes to the ever ongoing exploitation of the earth, and supernatural reality. In her lecture Marion Zimmer Bradley reveals some of the ideas that inspired her, and where she encountered them.

Richard Cavendish, the renowned author of "King Arthur and The Grail – The Arthurian Legends and their Meaning", was invited to conclude the symposium on The Vitality of the Arthurian Legend. In his lecture, "The Knight Errant: The Quest for Integrity", Mr. Cavendish delves beneath the surface of the Arthurian material and the textual problems and discusses the question: "What are the stories really about?" I think the readers will find that Richard Cavendish is touching upon some of the very essential themes of this very enduring and moving legend, when he chooses to draw attention to the emotional, philosophical, and psychological truths conveyed in it. Seeing that Dr. Graham Caie opened the symposium by talking about the human condition, it is fitting and appropriate that Richard Cavendish closes the proceedings by stressing this. The circle has come full.

It cannot be said that we have covered all the genres, fields, and countries of interest in the Arthurian material. Far from it. To quote Andrew Marvell: "had we but world enough, and time", it would have been wonderful to include specific papers on for instance Alfred Lord Tennyson and his "Idylls of the King", and "The Once and Future King" by T.H. White, not to mention the possibility of inviting more comtemporary writers of Arthurian fiction, such as Mary Stewart, Rosemary Sutcliff, Sharan Newman, Gillian Bradshaw, and Richard Monaco – all authors, who have helped convey the fascination of the Arthurian ideal. In an age that has "demythed" itself we turn to the past, and though we have long ago lost the illusion of "the just ruler", we still have a need to dream of one – maybe an example of "sophisticated" day-dreaming, which reveals that despite itself, mankind does have a potential for creating a dignified world, symbolizing what we could become, if we would sacrifice what we are – like the knight errant.

So, we proudly present our lecturers and "The Vitality of the Arthurian Legend"! The very vitality of the Matter of Britain is also reflected in its popularity in Denmark, though this country is not traditionally considered part of the

"Anglo-saxon" world of culture. However, Geoffrey of Monmouth claims that Denmark surrendered to King Arthur. He is right. Some of us certainly did!

Mette Pors, Research Fellow.

A City Built to Music: An Introduction to the Story of Arthur

By GRAHAM D. CAIE, *University of Copenhagen*

✠

"What place is there to which the winged praise of Arthur has not extended? Who is there that does not speak of Arthur of Britain?" asks the Prior of Tewkesbury in 1170, and mentions Asia, Egypt, Rome, Carthage and Palestine, indeed the whole known world, where Arthur is known. In Odense today this conference bears witness to the fact that he is as alive over eight hundred years later, and that he continues to inspire musicians, painters, novelists, poets, filmmakers and scholars. And the reason for this phenomenal success is something that we shall be discussing here. The International Arthur Society's bibliography lists thousands of items in its many volumes, as Arthur is big business in the academic world. The figure of Arthur himself and the geographic locations associated with the legend have evoked wide public interest. Authors such as Geoffrey Ashe have made exciting discoveries and made that pale figure that is briefly mentioned in the Annals come alive, while internationally famous novelists such as Marion Zimmer Bradley have demonstrated how the Arthurian myths are as popular today as they were 800 years ago and have much to teach our own era.

Arthur has inspired film-makers such as John Boorman with his *Excalibur* and Robert Bresson with his *Lancelot du Lac*, and of course the Monty Python gang had a field day with *The Holy Grail*. Classics such as T.H. White's *The Once and Future King* and Twain's *A Connecticut Yankee at King Arthur's Court* have given rise to musicals, such as *Camelot*. Then there are films and cartoons, such as Walt Disney's *The Sword in the Stone*, not to mention such unforgettable experiences as Bugs Bunny starring in *A Connecticut Rabbit in King Arthur's Court*. And finally one might mention the centuries of artists attracted to the legend all over the world, the best known probably those of the medieval revival of the 19th century: the Pre-Raphaelites, Rossetti, Morris and Burne-Jones, and others such as James Archer and Arthur Sandys.

An abbot in 1220 when finding his audience of monks asleep during his sermon woke them up, he tells us, by stating "And now I shall tell you of

Arthur!" And that is what I hope to attempt in the next few minutes: to try to keep you awake by talking about Arthur.

The story of Arthur is like a great and expanding city – a city built to music, Tennyson's Merlin suggests, and therefore never built at all, as it has no sound location in history, and yet it is built forever, as it cannot be destroyed except by lack of imagination. It is a city particularly congenial to those who believe in the power of the imagination and find hope in humanity, as it can be continually recreated by literary architects of vision and hope. It has been readily assimilated by rulers and politicians who have visions of the perfect society or who simply see themselves as enlightened rulers.

The city of Camelot is attractive to archaeologists and historians who want to dig into its prehistoric origins; it also attracts literary visitors who wish to admire its superb Norman, Gothic, Victorian and modern buildings. Most medieval legends are frozen in time, like Gothic cathedrals with only minor modern additions, while Camelot continues to expand and be modernized. As long as we have visionaries and prophets, people with dreams and hopes for a better society, then we will have Camelot, the city built to music. Richard Cavendish states that the central theme is "the search for integrity, the attempt to find and realize one's true and best self: 'ideal manhood closed in real man' ", he concludes, quoting Tennyson.

Arthur personifies whatever ideal the author wishes to promote, and in Arthur's city of Camelot we see society's attempt to realize that ideal. In the best of Arthurian legends the dream is impossible to fulfill for any length of time, largely because mankind neither can be nor should be ideal, as it is in human ambiguities and paradoxes that his strength and beauty lie: "a being dimly wise and rudely great". Alan Lupack, editor of *Avalon to Camelot*, states that "The Dream of Camelot, like the American Dream, is a glorious ideal which, though doomed to failure, is so noble that its failure is not pathetic but tragic." The Arthurian world is ... "one in which the dream of perfection is impossible to achieve because of its distance from the actual and the practical or, more simply, because of the demands of the the real world."

But why Arthur and not any other hero? Why should Arthur survive, having such obscure and flimsy beginnings and not a great hero like Alexander who was as popular in the Middle Ages? Perhaps the answer lies in the very fact that his origins are so vague.

The initial reason in the Middle Ages is probably political, or more precisely, nationalistic. Arthur is a British hero required to boost the ego of a continually conquered island. It is of course Geoffrey of Monmouth who with his *History of the Kings of Britain* in c. 1135 consciously fabricates a national hero to rival those in France and Italy, while at the same time giving the Welsh a national history equal to that presented by William of Malmesburg in his *Gesta Regum*

Anglorum (c. 1125). Geoffrey creates nearly a hundred kings from the fictitious Brutus of Troy and King Lear down to the seventh century Cadwallo. Arthur he makes the son of Uther Pendragon and Igerna, Duchess of Cornwall; with the help of Merlin the magician Uther deceives Igerna into thinking that he is Gorlois, Duke of Cornwall. Geoffrey locates the birth at Tintagel, as he particularly likes to give substance to his fictions by locating them in real places, such as Bath for the Battle of Badon or the river Camel in Cornwall or Caerleon. The Avalon that he mentions, however, is not located. Geoffrey took Nennius's character Ambrosius (in his *Historia Brittonum* of c. 800), who prophesied the victory of the Saxons over the Britons and merged it with the prophet Merlin. The mere mention of the name Mordred in connection with Arthur in the Easter Annals of the 6th century is expanded into the evil nephew, who forces Guinevere to marry him, creates civil war and dies in battle against Arthur at Camlann. Geoffrey also suggests the return of Arthur from Avalon which, in his later verse narrative *The Life of Merlin*, Geoffrey makes into a fairy island inhabited by mystic ladies, one of whom is Morgan le Fay and thereby preparing the scene for Marion Zimmer Bradley's masterpiece of a novel.

Loomis describes *The History of the Kings of Britain* as a great hoax, one of the world's most brazen and successful frauds and criticizes Geoffrey's impudence, thus echoing the criticism of Geoffrey's contemporaries that he wrote out of an inordinate love of lying or for the sake of pleasing the Britons. Richard Barber describes it as "romantic history" and suggests that the error lies with the early readers who wished to take it as historical fact. However one views it, the work was an overnight success, a best-seller of which there are over two hundred manuscript copies extant and which formed the basis of all later Arthurian Legends.

It flattered the Normans, giving them the illusion that they were the great conquerors of Europe and that their invasion of England was justified in Brutus who also brought a superior culture to the native inhabitants. There is no doubt that one of Geoffrey's major aims was personal promotion in the church now ruled by Norman bishops. On the other hand the defeated English nation could see Arthur as belonging to the losing side and the story gave the Britons and ironically those of Saxon origin a splendid heritage as well as preserving many of their myths and legends.

But such fiction could only have been so popular if it hit the right political note and been actively encouraged by the rulers. And so it has been throughout the ages: President Kennedy made allusions to the myth and most leaders see themselves as knights in shining armour saving their people from their evil opponents. Richard I, Edward I, Edward III and his son the Black Prince all claimed descent from Arthur: Henry II and Edward I had the Glastonbury tomb of Arthur opened to convince the Welsh that their hero was indeed dead and could not return to save them. Edward had the bones placed in a black marble tomb before the main altar where it remained until the Reformation, and he quoted Geoffrey to support his claim to the Scottish throne. He established a tournament of the Mensa Rotunda at which the combatants took the names of Arthur's knights.

Similarly when the Welsh Henry Tudor usurped the throne of England the story of Arthur was at its height. Henry insisted that he was descended from Arthur, named his heir apparent Arthur, and genealogies helpfully appeared to support this claim. Henry VIII and Elizabeth I continued to encourage the Tudor link with Arthur and royal pageants, masques and other drama took the Matter of Britain as their theme. The Round Table in the Great Hall of Winchester Castle, probably made in the time of Edward III, was painted in Henry's time with Tudor Roses, as well as a portrait of Arthur and the names of his knights. Other examples include the Earl of Leicester's masque, the play *The Misfortunes of Arthur* in 1587 by Thomas Hughes and of course Spenser's *Fairy Queen* in which Elizabeth I is Gloriana, Arthur's Queen. The Stuart dynasty continued this trend with James VI and I making much of the fact that he was the first king after Arthur to rule a united kingdom; Ben Jonson diplomatically hails James as a second Arthur in *The Masque of Oberon*. And so monarchs throughout the ages complimented themselves by claiming Arthurian descent and found "historical proof" for their claims on neighbouring territory. Even Victoria basked in Tennyson's allusions to Albert and herself as Arthur and Guinevere in his *The Idylls of the King* dedicated to the memory of Albert who

"seems to me
Scarce other than my king's ideal knight,...
Who loved only one and who clave to her –"

Luckily he downplayed the role of Guinevere in the comparison!

Authors can also turn the legend into political complaint, as the fourteenth-century author of the alliterative *Morthe Arthure* appears to criticize the drawn-out campaigns in the Hundred Years' War against France, or T.H. White, writing this century in the middle of a world war, makes the necessity of educating the next generation in the ways of peace his major theme.

And so the legend took root in political, specifically nationalistic, soil and flattered the English audience that they were the inheritors of a long and noble native dynasty rooted in Troy that could compare with the pedigrees of France and Italy. Alexander or other continental heroes could never have done that.

With the firm hold of the legend by the 12th century it experienced a second piece of good luck: the most important genre of the Middle Ages, the romance, adopted and adapted the myth and made Arthur synonymous with romance and with it the entire elaborate social and moral code of the medieval aristocracy and gentry. The Norman poet Wace, in the court of Eleanor of Aquitaine, wife of Henry II of England, wrote the *Roman de Brut* in 1155, based on Geoffrey and in French verse, intended for, as he states, "Rich Folk who possess revenue and silver, since for them books are made and good words composed and well set forth." Arthur loses the Rambo-like Germanic warrior's face and takes on that of French nobility; he is, states Wace, "one of Love's lovers: a lover also of glory; ... He ordained the courtesies of courts, and observed high state in a very splendid fashion." He creates a Guinevere in the model of the perfect lady of courtly love and it is Wace who introduces the Round Table.

With Chrétien de Troyes in the twelfth century the transformation of the Matter of Britain is complete. Chrétien merged old and new ideals, the heroic with the chivalric, and the new courtly code of manners and love, but above all he stressed the human element, and, writing at a time of humanistic renaissance, he stressed the role of the individual, giving individual knights the chance to prove themselves and their values outside the protection of the fellowship and away from Camelot. They set out on individual moral and spiritual journeys in search of personal fulfilment, and it is particularly in this context that the Grail Quest plays an important role.

Chrétien gave the aristocracy a medium in which to discuss their ideals and social concerns. It is not escapist literature for the idle rich, but presents vital issues such as feudal obligations, and mutual love as opposed to marriage while attempting to harmonize heroic ideals with the new code of courtly love. At the same time he manages to interweave the rich matter of Celtic lore: it was the French romance poets who introduced the Tristran and Iseult myth into the Arthurian matter, a myth with origins amongst the Celts; they also developed the complexities of the Grail legend, not always aware of the significance or symbolism of the matter. And it was a Burgundian knight, Robert de Boron, who was to develop the myth and connect it with Joseph of Arimathia, thereby making it possible for Glastonbury to claim the privilege of receiving Christ's chalice. And so Arthur flourished because of the needs of an age in France, Germany and Britain, and with the close political and social connections between France and Britain at this time the romances swiftly crossed to and fro over the Channel. In spite of Layamon's attempts when adapting Wace into English in his *Brut* (c. 1205) to turn him back again into a Germanic, bloody warrior, the romance figure of the flower of chivalry was permanently connected with Arthur. Perhaps the death of the romance in the post-medieval period hastened if not the disappearance at least the drop in popularity of Arthur on the Continent from the fifteenth century onwards, so closely was he part and parcel of the genre.

But in England of the fourteenth and fifteenth centuries Arthur was still needed as a national hero; he became a major figure in the alliterative revival that partially was the result of strong nationalistic feeling in the fourteenth century and regional desire to return to native themes and verse forms.

With Malory the Matter of Britain takes the form that most people know today. Malory in his c. 1469 *Le Morte D'Arthur* takes the vast and unwieldy French Vulgate Cycle and to it adds many other sources such as the Alliterative *Morthe Arthure* of the 14th century and gives the legend coherence. Malory's strength is in his ability to describe narrative in direct and uncomplicated prose; he seems uneasy with the spiritual dimensions in the Holy Grail and omits much of the exposition of the doctrine of grace and the moralizing that he found in his French source. The Grail Quest becomes yet another chivalrous mission in the vocation of knighthood which was Malory's major theme. Loomis calls him "a well-intentioned, honest, righteous man and a true gentleman with a strong sense of the realities of life and the human and practical side of things." Although Lancelot upstages Arthur in Malory's version, Malory is rather uneasy – like most English authors – with the passionate, romantic dimension in which the French sources delighted and made Lancelot the central figure. Perhaps it is an English failing to be embarrassed by passion!

Like a blushing school boy confronted by a passionate woman, Lancelot is totally confused when asked by the Fair Damsel why he does not marry: "then I must ... leave arms and tournaments, battles and adventures. And as for ... paramours", he exclaims horrified, "that woll I refuse: in principal for dread of God, ... for then they be not happy neither fortunate unto the wars." Girls, then, seem to spoil the boys' games and possibly bring bad luck, and there is no question of whether love or war comes first. What attracts Malory to the figure of Lancelot is his loyalty, courtesy, faithfulness and valour: he is a man of integrity who commands the esteem of his fellow knights, and yet is sufficiently human to allow himself to be betrayed by his emotions concerning Guinevere, although the love affair is greatly modified by Malory.

It is Malory's version of the major events of the legend that finds its way into later works: the sword in the stone, the receiving of Excalibur from the Lady of the Lake, the morbid story of Arthur's slaughter of the children born on May Day in an attempt to kill Mordred, the tragedy of the brothers Balin and Balan killing each other without knowing their true identity and the infatuation of Merlin for Nimue. But his masterpiece of invention is the final battle and the death of Arthur: "Comfort thyself," said the king, "and do as well as thou mayest, for in me is no trust for to trust in. For I must into the vale of Avilion to heal me of my grievous wound. And if you hear never more of me, pray for my soul." And so the three queens receive him onto the barge and he floats out of sight. Yet, adds Malory, "some men say in many parts of England that King Arthur is not dead, but had by the will of our Lord Jesu into another place; and men say that he shall come again, and he shall win the holy cross." And thus the myth of the eternal return is grafted onto the Arthur story.

But we must never forget that a major reason for the survival of Arthur is the simple and basic appeal of the legends to all age groups. Stories of adventure, intrigue, conflict of loyalties, magic and myth and love and passion. Caxton describes Malory's works as "many joyous and playsaunt historyes and noble and renomed actes of humanyté, gentylnesse, and chyvalryes." He printed the tales because "many noble and diverse gentlemen of this realm of England" had expressed a wish to read of "the most renowned Christian king, ... King Arthur, which ought most to be remembered amongst us Englishmen before all other Christian kings." Many believe that the relics clearly show his existence, states Caxton – the tomb at Glastonbury, the print of his seal in the shrine of Edward the Confessor, the skull of Gawain at Dover Castle, the Round Table at Winchester and Lancelot's sword.

Many, it would appear, looked on the romances as popular, escapist literature, especially those of Lancelot and Guinevere: Chaucer mocks the

> "Book of Launcelot du Lac
> That women holde in full gret reverence"

while it was the same book that led to the passion and consequent damnation of poor Francesca and Paulo in Dante's *Inferno*:

> "One day we read for pastime how in thrall
> Lord Lancelot lay in love, who loved the Queen;
> We were alone – we thought no harm at all
> ... we read no more that day!"

But the triumph of Arthur through the centuries and definitely in post medieval times must be its adaptability as a vehicle for visionary ideas. As long as people have visions, imagination and dreams, we will have Arthur: as long as we have scholars interested in the mentality of a specific age, we will have Arthurian scholarship. Geoffrey and Layamon give us the fierce Germanic face, just as the Anglo-Saxons made their Christ the conquering prince. We create our God and our Arthur in our own image – that of our age and that of our personal vision – and reflect the hopes and fears of that new age. And so the face changes from the mild, romantic lover of the romance to the morally confused and generally misunderstood Arthur of Tennyson and T.H. White, reflecting perhaps their own personal tensions and problems, but also what they considered the corruption and social disintegration and fragmentation of their times. Twain is worried about the social consequences of the new technology, while Marion Bradley voices the concerns of 20th century women through the mists of the legend. The legend is the vehicle and as it has the proportions of major myth, it can adapt to the message. The best authors are those like White and Bradley who, like Merlin, make their ideas available, allow us to see them in function and even to discuss their shortcomings. They suggest the potential for an improved society.

The story provides a mythology as complex and profound as Christianity. It presents a mystical king of extraordinary origins who "from the great deep to the great deep he goes": a king who brings the message of a new society and creates order, harmony, and cosmos, who inspires his followers and makes a closely-knit fellowship of apostles and who dies for his people promising to return and save them.

But Arthur is very much an incarnate god, a god of this world, who promises no after-life, no solutions for eternal peace: he is the saviour of the humanist, who shows how man can and must use his human potential to improve his social and moral position. The myth allows us to see how, for a brief period, such a brave new world can be created, and also warns us that, because of the innate tension between ideals and emotions, how it is bound to failure. The Arthurian vision is cyclical, as is the story of humanity, and it is not by chance that Tennyson links his *Idylls* to the changing seasons of the year. Every generation must create its own ideals, must try to implement them, and must know that it can never reach perfection, but nonetheless will achieve heights of human dignity in its attempts to approximate it.

> And slowly answer'd Arthur from the barge;
> "The old order changeth, yielding place to new,
> And God fulfils himself in many ways,
> Lest one good custom should corrupt the world."

It is the process and possibly the struggle, then, not the success of achievement that becomes the goal. White shows the problems involved in Camelot once Wart's vision of Civilisation has been achieved. He has now a bunch of unemployed and thus potentially dangerous knights on his hands and has to think up the Quest for the Grail as a Labour Incentive Scheme: "I suppose all endeavours which are directed to a purely worldly end, as my famous Civilization was, contain within themselves the germs of their own corruption, " states Wart, "and as people reach perfection, they disappear." And so he sends them packing on a futile quest, although one dreadful thought plagues Arthur – what if someone actually were to find God!! And the perfect in any case are insufferable:

> "I don't hold it against Galahad for being a virgin, but don't you think that people might be a little human?... Why couldn't he say Good-morning or something, instead of rescuing a fellow and then riding away in silence with that white nose of his in the air?"

We fail because of the human condition, says White, "But failure builds success and nature changes. A good man's example always does instruct the ignorant and lessens their rage, little by little through the ages, until the spirit of the waters is content..."

It is only for a space, Tennyson states, that the beast can be held at bay:

> Arthur ..."slew the beast, and fell'd
> The forest, letting in the sun ...
> And all men's hearts became
> Clean for a season."

More no man can achieve, and if he thinks he can permanently live up to the code of absolutes, then he deceives himself. The laughter at the court of King Arthur when Gawain in *Sir Gawain and the Green Knight* returns is not mockery, but relief that Gawain is but human. Gawain's fault is his pride in thinking that he could live a perfect life according to both Christian and courtly codes. Being a little less than an angel yet more than the beast creates both the complexities, ambiguities and confusions of man in a middle state while at the same time forming a human being that is attractive and delightfully unpredictable. In Christianity this paradox is expressed in the concept of the fortunate fall – "Blessed be the apple!" states a medieval lyric. The story of Arthur, then, is the perfect vehicle to convey the complexities and paradoxes of the human condition and it was initially this legend that Milton considered sufficiently elevated and all-embracing for the great epic he planned that would justify God's ways to man.

Tennyson creates his Arthur and Guinevere as "the fair beginners of a nobler time" like prelapsarian Adam and Eve. They built a fair new world, Camelot, built to music and many knights are entranced by the euphoria created by Arthur's vision. They are like keen apostles of a new religion, swearing vows

> "Of utter hardiness, utter gentleness,
> And, loving, utter faithfulness in love,
> And uttermost obedience to the king."

It works – for a space – and then the inevitable disillusionment, expressed by a cynical but realistic Tristram:

> " – The vows!
> O, ay – the wholesome madness of an hour –
> They served their use, their time; for every knight
> Believed himself a greater than himself."

Surely the humanist can expect no more than this just exploitation of mans potential. But for those who feel and require human love, the strain of the vows is overwhelming and conflict of loyalties creeps in. Poor Guinevere finds life with the utterly perfect man unbearable:

> She broke into a little scornful laugh:
> "Arthur, my lord, Arthur, the faultless King,
> That passionate perfection, my good lord –
> But who can gaze upon the Sun in heaven?
>   ... to me
> He is all fault who hath no fault at all.
> For who loves me must have a touch of earth;"

And so the old order changeth, giving place to new, when that great cause of Arthur's begins to corrupt. But at the tragic end there is still a gleam of hope: "And the new sun rose bringing the new year."

Surely in this symposium we will show that Tennyson is right when he states: "There is no grander subject in the world than King Arthur."

Works cited

Alcock, Leslie. *Arthur' Britain*. Penguin Books, Harmondsworth, 1973.
Ashe, Geoffrey. ed. *The Quest for Arthur's Britain*. Pall Mall Press, London, 1968.
-- --. *Camelot and the Vision of Albion*. Heinemann, London, 1971.
Barber, Richard. *King Arthur: Hero and Legend*. Boydell Press, Ipswich, 3rd. ed., 1986.
-- --. *The Knight and Chivalry*. Longman, London, 1970.
Bradley, Marion Zimmer. *The Mists of Avalon*. Sphere Books, London, 1984.
Brengle, Richard L. ed. *Arthur – King of Britain*. Prentice-Hall, Inc., New Jersey, 1964.
Cavendish, Richard. *King Arthur and the Grail*. Paladin, London, 1980.
Comfort, W.W. ed. *Chretien de Troyes' Arthurian Romances*. J.M. Dent, London, 1914, rpt. 1967.
Geoffrey of Monmouth. *The History of the Kings of Britain*, ed. L. Thorpe, Penguin Books, Harmondsworth, 1966.
Jenkins, Elizabeth. *The Mystery of King Arthur*. Coward, McCann & Geoghegan, New York, 1975.
Loomis, R.S. *The Development of Arthurian Romance*. Hutchinson, London, 1963.
-- --. The Grail: *From Celtic Myth to Christian Symbol*. Columbia University Press, New York, 1963.

Lupack, Alan. "Merlin in America", *Arthurian Interpretations 1* (1986), 64-74.
Malory, Sir Thomas. *Works*, ed. Eugene Vinaver, 3 vols., Clarendon Press, Oxford, 2nd ed., 1973.
Pors, Mette. "From a Troubled Heart": A Reading of T.H. White's *The Once and Future King*. Unpublished thesis, Copenhagen, 1982.
Ricks, Christopher. *The Poems of Tennyson*. Longman, London, 1969.
Tolkien, J.R.R. and Gordon, E.V. eds. *Sir Gawain and The Green Knight*, Clarendon Press, Oxford, 1952.
Warner, Sylvia Townsend. *T.H. White: A Biography*. Jonathan Cape, London, 1967.
White, T.H. *The Once and Future King*. Fontana, Collins, London, 1967.

The Historical Origins of the Arthurian Legend

By GEOFFREY ASHE

✠

In choosing a title I have avoided that well-worn phrase "the historical Arthur". It implies a mode of approach which I now believe to be inadequate, even fallacious. Scholars in quest of such a person have tried to find him by stripping away legend and isolating hard evidence. In practice this has meant dismissing the medieval literature, delving back behind it to earlier matter of Welsh provenance, and picking out supposedly trustworthy statements. The statements that have been claimed as trustworthy are few. They are confined, or almost confined, to a couple of Latin texts containing brief records of battles Arthur is said to have fought as a British war-leader, chiefly to wipe out encroaching Saxons. One is the *Historia Brittonum*, History of the Britons, compiled early in the ninth century and ascribed, dubiously, to a monk of Bangor named Nennius. The other is a chronicle, the *Annales Cambriae* or Annals of Wales, which is somewhat later. After many years of discussion, I think it must be confessed that their curt Arthurian notices do not lead reliably to a real Arthur.

Nothing in these can be proved close enough in date to his reputed *floruit* as a Briton of the post-Roman period. Even if we honestly try to accept them, despite the long interval, they raise chronological problems of their own. They spread out Arthur's activities over such a span of time that he would have had to fight his last battle as a centenarian or nearly so. To make this point is not to indulge in a hypercritical modern quibble; it was realized by at least two medieval authors. We might hope to pin him down in some specific part of the time-range, but this cannot be done, because we are never given a chronological fix relating him to known history. We get a couple of alleged dates – which are quite irreconcilable with other clues – but we are not told that his first battle took place when So-and so was emperor, or his last when So-and-so was pope. He drifts in a temporal void.

There is a further crux. His crowning victory is stated to have been the battle of Badon. This was an actual battle, but when the *Historia* credits him with killing 960 Saxons at it single-handed, in one charge, it is clear that he has already become legendary. Badon as an event really involving him, and to some extent the whole series, must therefore be called in question. Historians have been right to exclude what is said of him in other Welsh matter, in the penumbra of saga comprising poems and tales, and episodes in fabulous "lives" of saints. But even when they have set all that aside, and concentrated on the battles in the two quasi-historical texts, thet have not really got rid of legend. Even there, the difference is of degree rather than kind. One *Annales* entry about the "strife of Camlann" has been held up as a plain historical statement, free from legend, but to make Arthur's existence depend on this raises such difficulties in other quarters that I would not care to build on it.[1]

The failure of the "historical Arthur" approach is exposed by the contradictions of those who have tried it. Some make Arthur a national leader, some a regional one. Some make him a belated emperor, some a king, some a general, some a semi-barbaric minor chief. Some put him in the south, some in Wales, some in the north. And so on. A method that produces such discrepant results is self-refuted.

I am not contending that the testimony of the two texts is worthless. Arthur's battles, or some of them, may be authentic. The man sketchily portrayed fighting them may be real. I do say that no certainty can be reached by the Welsh route, that it never leads to a convincingly documented figure. Plainly Arthur became a popular hero with Welsh bards and story-tellers – Cornish and Breton ones, too – and made a powerful, eventually dominant impression before medieval romancers took him up. It is natural to feel that there must have been somebody behind it all, and the feeling may be right. That has always been my personal view, at least to the extent that it is easier on balance to believe in such a person than to disbelieve, and it is my view still. But the fact must be faced, inference from a hero's saga to his existence is hazardous. In the United States, tall tales and wonderful exploits were associated with the folk-heroes Davy Crockett and Paul Bunyan. While Davy Crockett did exist, Paul Bunyan did not. Or to cite a more recent cautionary instance, Sherlock Holmes is so vivid that many people have thought him real, and fan-clubs have solemnly debated such questions as whether he went to Oxford or Cambridge. (It was Oxford, by the way, though the incident proving it has gone almost unremarked.) New Holmes stories continue to be invented, new films continue to be made. Yet we know how the saga began, and it was not in the career of an actual detective, but in a novelist's imagination.

With Arthur I would ask, not directly "Did he exist?" but "How did the legend originate, what facts is it rooted in?" To do so is to cast the net wider, with the understanding that it may finally haul in a real person, but may not. Obviously Arthur was, to coin a word, mythified, like Davy Crockett and much more so. Yet before launching on the inquiry, I suggest that despite the ambiguity of the Welsh clues we have several reasons for suspecting a real person rather than one who is entirely imaginary. If, on other grounds, an Arthur-figure shows signs of emerging, they will add to his credibility as the source of inspiration.

First, all the persons mentioned in the *Annales Cambriae*, outside the Arthur entries, do seem to be real. Therefore those entries are likely to reflect some sort of human reality. A completely mythical Arthur would be out of keeping with the character of the chronicle.

Then there is the name. "Arthur" is a Welsh form of the Roman "Artorius." It suggests a Briton born when the island was still under Roman influence and parents were giving their children Roman names. It does not suggest a Celtic fairy-tale character, or a fictitious chief invented by some Cymric bard hundreds of years later. Furthermore, with this particular name, something unusual happened. It enjoyed a sudden, unprecedented vogue in the second half of the sixth century, when several Arthurs are on record up and down Britain. They are best explained as having been called after a single famous one who was already an established hero of song and story. All this accords with Arthur's reputed post-Roman *floruit*.[2]

Then again, a motif that looks utterly mythical does in fact favour historicity. This is the cave-legend. According to ancient popular lore, Arthur is still living and will some day return, and one version of the belief affirms that he lies asleep in a cave. When collecting material for a guidebook I found that he lies asleep in at least fifteen caves. Nevertheless, the folklorist Jennifer Westwood has pointed out an aspect of the cave-legend that is easily missed. During the Middle Ages and afterwards, much the same is told of other national heroes across Europe, such as Frederick Barbarossa; and while the theme may have a remote ancestry in Celtic myth, it does not attach itself to purely fairy-tale characters. In every case the sleeper is conceived as a human being with a known historical context, and in a large majority of cases he actually is historical, however transformed by his strange condition. Therefore the sleeper called Arthur is likely to be historical himself, or, at any rate, to incorporate a tradition of someone who was.[3]

The final point is negative, yet it carries weight. No one who has definitely denied Arthur has succeeded in accounting for the phenomenon without him. Incantatory repetition of words like "myth" is mere evasion. If there was no Arthur at all, what did happen, where did the idea of him come from, what started the story, and when and why? Attempts have been made to explain him as a Celtic god "euhemerized" into a larger-than-life human. A few Celtic deities, such as Bran, underwent this treatment in early literature, but there is no relevant instance of such a deity being given a quasi-biography in a specific and fairly recent historical setting. "Artorius" could scarcely be the name of a Celtic god, and no document or inscription witnesses to a pre-Christian deity with a name that could have generated "Arthur" in some other way. A theory that the supposed god was a late-comer to the pantheon, the divine patron of a post-Roman patriotic revival of the old religion, comes to grief on the well-known tract of Gildas in the sixth century. Gildas denounces his British fellow-Christians for just about every sin, except apostasy. He would have denounced neo-paganism if there had been any.

In the upshot, advocates of a divine or purely mythical Arthur have refuted themselves, both by misrepresentation of fact in the interests of theory, and by mutual contradictions worse than those of the "historical Arthur" school. The image of a human being with a solidity resisting their exorcism emerges, if dimly, by default.

In probing the legend more precisely for origins, we confront a daunting obstacle. Not only is most of what is related of Arthur unhistorical, it is peculiarly baffling for the present purpose, because so much of it takes the form of medieval romance. Medieval romancers, unlike modern historical novelists, care little for authenticity. When they draw on themes from the distant past – on the cycle of the Trojan War or the deeds of Alexander – they update freely. Their tales of Arthur are no exception. Chrétien de Troyes and the rest present him so as to interest their public, which is aristocratic or upper-middle-class. Arthur becomes the monarch of a chivalric Utopia. He presides over an elegant court and an order of knights wearing sophisticated armour, in a milieu of castles and tournaments, heraldry and courtly love. Is there any way down from this gorgeous edifice to its deep and secret foundations? and even if there is, how to find it, when the Welsh tradition is a dead end?

A question worth asking is how the romancers, and their readers and listeners, saw the issue themselves. Most of them probably regarded Arthur's kingdom somewhat as we regard the Wild West. We know that the West actually was wild for a few decades, that there were cowboys and Indians and sheriffs, that persons such as Billy the Kid and Calamity Jane existed. On the other hand, unless we have a special interest in that period, it doesn't matter much. The Wild West is a realm of the imagination, created by novelists like Owen Wister and Zane Grey, and then by Hollywood: a realm where certain kinds of adventure take place. The whole scene has been transformed into a national myth. Yet even though its factual basis isn't the point, it does have one. Likewise, for most medieval people who cared about Arthur at all, it was the stories they cared about. Yet they would have agreed that in some cloudy antiquity, he did exist.

That belief disposes of any notion that we are misguidedly seeking fact behind a romantic literature known to be fancy. It was not. The chief reason for the belief in Arthur was that he had been given an official biography, supplying a framework into which the romances more or less fitted. As a quasi-historical ruler over Britain, he was the creation of one man. Towards 1138 – perhaps a trifle later (it now appears) than some scholars have thought, but the margin of doubt is only a matter of a couple of years – Geoffrey of Monmouth published his *Historia Regum Britanniae*, History of the Kings of Britain.[4]

This mis-named work is one of the most important books of the Middle Ages, the source of other stories besides Arthur's, that of King Lear, for instance. It begins in the twelfth century B.C. with an expanded version of a Welsh legend telling how the island, then called Albion, was settled by migrating Trojans under the leadership of Brutus, Aeneas's great-grandson. It was re-named Britain in his honour. Geoffrey goes on to narrate a long series of fictitious reigns, and makes out that the line of British kings persisted even through the period of Roman rule, which he cuts down to a vague protectorate: he accommodates several emperors to his scheme by portraying them as Britons or demi-Britons or Britons-by-marriage.

After the island's separation from the Empire, his story moves through several decades to an Arthurian climax. He tells how an unscrupulous noble called Vortigern usurped the throne and invited a mob of heathen Saxons, led by Hengist, to make their homes in Britain as auxiliary troops in his own service. Thousands more arrived and they got out of hand, overrunning parts of the country. Vortigern fled to Wales, where Merlin prophesied his downfall. Soon afterwards the rightful princes, two brothers, returned from exile and overthrew him. The elder was succeeded after a short reign by the younger, Uther Pendragon. Both managed to contain the Saxons but neither could deliver a knockout blow. Geoffrey introduces Arthur, King Uther's son, as a kind of Messiah restoring stability and rescuing Britain from its troubles.

His tale of Arthur's origin is well known. Part of its interest lies in the role of Merlin, which supplies the first hint for his prominence in Arthur's regime as depicted by romancers, and for the idea of its having a supernatural dimension. Uther, we are told, conceived an ungovernable desire for Ygerna, the wife of Gorlois, duke of Cornwall. A conflict resulted in which the king's soldiers fought the duke's. To put his wife out of Uther's reach, Gorlois immured her in his castle of Tintagel, on a rocky headland accessible only by way of a narrow isthmus – today, a bridge. But Merlin magically changed Uther into a replica of the duke, and in that effective disguise he passed the guards, climbed the steps, entered the castle, and had his way with Ygerna. In the film *Excalibur* Uther goes through this procedure wearing full medieval armour, a feat implying much exertion on his part and much discomfort on hers. Thus was Arthur begotten. As Gorlois had conveniently fallen in battle, the king could resume his true shape and make Ygerna his queen, with an heir whose paternity was in no doubt.

Arthur, Geoffrey continues, came to the throne while very young but soon proved himself a brilliant leader, subduing the Saxons in Britain, crushing the Picts and Scots who aided them, conquering Ireland, and, as an afterthought, conquering Iceland (which would not then have presented much difficulty, because it was uninhabited). He married Guinevere, and reigned in peace and prosperity for twelve years, loved and respected by his subjects. During this time he founded an order of knighthood enrolling men of note from all countries. He then conquered Norway and Denmark and invaded Gaul, still shakily held by the Roman Empire, annexing large portions of it and allotting governorships to his knights Kay and Bedivere.

Britain now stood at an apogee of wealth, power and culture. In another phase of peace Arthur held court magnificently at Caerleon-upon-Usk in Wales. When the Roman ruler Lucius demanded tribute and a restitution of conquests, he took an army to Gaul again leaving his nephew Mordred (the romancers' spelling; Geoffrey's is "Modred") in charge at home, jointly with Guinevere. He won a decisive battle in the neighbourhood of the land of the Allobroges, i.e. Burgundy, and pressed on into that part of the country. News from Britain recalled him. Mordred had turned traitor, proclaimed himself king, and made a deal with the Saxons. Arthur hastened home and defeated him in Cornwall, but was gravely wounded himself and taken away to the Isle of Avalon – *Insula Avallonis* – for his wounds to be attended to. Geoffrey leaves the door open for the folk-belief in Arthur's immortality and destined return, without asserting it himself. The King simply departs in the direction of Avalon, unlocated, with no recorded death. Afterwards the *History* traces the Britons' decline till they maintain their identity only fragmentarily in the west, as Welsh, and the English descendants of the Saxons have triumphed.

Where did Geoffrey get all this? The little that is known of him does not help much. He was a cleric, and was teaching at Oxford from 1129 to 1151. There he made the acquaintance of Walter, Oxford's archdeacon. He claims in a preface that the *History* is translated or adapted from "a certain very ancient book written in the British language" which Walter gave him. The British language, in this context, could mean Welsh but is more likely to mean Breton, the closely-related speech of the people of Brittany, descendants of emigrants from Britain in the fifth and sixth centuries. Geoffrey himself seems to have been of Welsh or Breton stock, but it is not possible to be sure which. His claim about the book is incredible as it stands. There may, however, have been a lost Breton source for some of his work, perhaps giving information or pseudo-information on Arthur, who figures in the traditions of Brittany as well as Wales.[5]

If we go through Geoffrey's work comparing it with known history, we can see that it presents a bewildering problem. Where it can be checked, as in the

Roman period, the prevalence of fiction is manifest. Geoffrey is not a historian and can never be trusted for facts. Yet he cannot be dismissed as a sheer fantasist either. Except in some of the fabulous early reigns he normally *uses* history or what he would like to think is history, drawing on Roman authors, on Gildas, on Bede, on the *Historia Brittonum*, and doing it with attention and skill. He inflates, he inverts, he confounds chronology, he perpetrates all manner of outrages, but he hardly ever invents substantial episodes out of nothing at all. Even when his story is legendary, as in most of the sections dealing with Vortigern, the legends are not fabrications of his own, they are based on older Welsh matter. Even in the Tintagel affair, archaeology has shown that he is using a tradition of the place's importance at about the right time. It is futile to look in his work, however selectively, for real history, but it is proper to ask what themes he may be drawing from real history for his literary creation.

During the post-Roman phase in general, he plainly has some inkling of realities, however wildly he dramatizes and falsifies. First, as to dating: Britain's separation from Rome, the family relationships of the kings, a reference to a known British visitation by Gallic bishops in 429, and the continued existence of a sort of emperor in the west, combine to prove that in contriving the story's main structure as far as Arthur's demise he meant it all to happen in the fifth century, whatever doubt he may have sown by retouching and second thoughts. It is only fair to mention that the *History* gives a date for the demise, 542. However, it is so blatantly inconsistent that it is probably an error. This point is more than wishful thinking and I will come back to it.

Within the fifth-century range, several of the major characters are based, however loosely, on persons whom history attests. The overall situation is rightly conceived. Britain with its Celtic inhabitants, ancestors of the Welsh, did drift free of the Empire about 410. The Anglo-Saxons, ancestors of the English, did cross the North Sea and settle as *foederati* or auxiliaries, many, probably, under the auspices of a ruler known as Vortigern, which means "over-chief" and denotes a Briton comparable to an Irish high king, paramount over regional rulers. He figures in the *Historia Brittonum* as an arch-villain. The settlers did receive reinforcements and get out of hand, somewhere about the middle of the century. After extensive raiding over a longish period they withdrew to their authorized enclaves and were contained for a time by British counter-action, led partly or wholly by a certain Ambrosius Aurelianus, a commander, not a king, perhaps in the service of a successor of Vortigern.The unique Arthurian legend which Geoffrey gives such grandiose form is rooted in a unique train of events, which has been called the "Arthurian Fact," meaning the fact of history which Arthur came to symbolize, whether he existed or not. Alone among the Empire's provincial peoples, the Britons achieved *de facto* independence before the barbarians advanced, fought back when they did, and, for some decades, brought the situation more or less under control, with most of the ex-Roman territory still in British hands.

Geoffrey is aware of that recovery. He inflates it into an Arthurian revolution. The nature of that revolution, largely fanciful as it is, has its interest. While he updates to a large extent, as the romancers do, his Arthur is not so much a model medieval sovereign as a British version of a ruler yearned for during the troubles of the later Empire: the *Restitutor Orbis* or World-Restorer, the emperor who would end internal warfare and usurpation, master the barbarians, conquer foreign enemies, and reinstate a long-lost peace and prosperity. Once or twice in the fourth century the thing almost seemed to be happening, and although the hope finally expired in the west, it survived till near the end. Somehow Geoffrey has a feeling for the atmosphere of that time, for its ideals and aspirations, and his Messianic Arthur is a *Restitutor* for Britain, still part of the imperial world. If his conception has literary antecedents in this respect, they are in the panegyrics of Sidonius Apollinaris, who, during the 450s and 60s, hailed each of three transitory emperors as the saviour of Rome and civilization.[6]

But where, specifically, does Geoffrey's story of Arthur come from? Some of it comes from the Welsh items already mentioned, the two texts recording his battles, or something like them. But these account for only about one-fifth of it, and the emphasis is entirely changed. His victories over the Saxons, which are the whole point of his career in the Nennian battle-list, become merely a preface to the deeds that really matter. When Geoffrey deals with the villain of Welsh tradition, Vortigern, he simply expands what that tradition supplies. When he deals with the hero, Arthur, he does something quite different. More than half the story is taken up with Arthur's warfare in Gaul. Assessed by allocation of space, and by the climactic order, Geoffrey's King is more a Gallic conqueror than anything else. Nor is this an aberration that disappears later. Romancers, such as Chrétien de Troyes and Wolfram von Eschenbach, accept the importance of his continental domain and portray him holding court in Brittany.

Significant too is Geoffrey's treatment of the King's passing. When he first foreshadows this, in a prophecy uttered by Merlin, he seems to picture it happening in Gaul. When he comes to compose the actual account of it, he does use the Welsh story of the "strife of Camlann" in which Arthur fought Medraut, the original Mordred. But he still has the disaster strike while Arthur is overseas, and he superimposes a wholly un-Welsh theme, turning Mordred into a deputy-ruler who betrays Arthur and conspires with barbarians. It may be noteworthy that in the only passage where he says anything specific about his alleged source, the British book, he claims that it informed him about the circumstances of Arthur's downfall.[7]

Here, I believe, is the point where "historical Arthur" investigators have missed the way. Whatever else they have judged worth pursuing, they have been virtually unanimous in dismissing Arthur's Gallic activities as pure fantasy on Geoffrey's part. It follows, or is assumed to follow, that the only real evidence for him must be in Britain, meaning in practice Wales, and the inquiry is steered to an inconclusive result. Geoffrey's tale of imperial involvements in Gaul is not history. But if we are to reject it as totally baseless, we have to suppose that he is doing here what he does not do anywhere else, from Julius Caesar onward –inventing a very long, very important episode (to be precise, two linked instalments of such an episode) out of nothing whatsoever; not so much as a hint. That cannot be said even of his account of Arthur's knighthood and court. While the court is medieval, the essential notion of Arthur's having one, with a large array of followers, was established in Wales – as the tale *Culhwch and Olwen* shows – long before Geoffrey wrote. But, for the idea of an embroilment in the affairs of Gaul and the western Empire, Wales supplies nothing.

Must we admit that this is indeed an exception, that Geoffrey raises the King to his height of glory with a prolonged and irresponsible flight of fancy, unparalleled in the parts of his book preceding and following? Some years ago I challenged the academic assumption, and began to notice curious things.

First, a surprising piece of exactitude. I mentioned a serious drawback with the Welsh matter, its failure to provide Arthur with a chronological fix, lining him up with known history. But Geoffrey's Gallic narrative does. Three times he tells us that when Arthur was in Gaul, the emperor – evidently the eastern one at Constantinople – was Leo. This has to be Leo I, who reigned from 457 to 474. Here we not only have a chronological fix, as desired, we have the only one that Arthur gets anywhere up to Geoffrey's time.

That is not all. During the first Gallic campaign, Leo seems to have no western colleague and to be sole emperor. There actually was an interregnum when this was so. During the second, greater campaign, he does have a western colleague, the Lucius who provokes it by making unwise demands on Arthur. Lucius's status is imprecise. Geoffrey introduces him as "Procurator of the Republic" and depicts the Senate as having power to give him orders – touches suggesting a vague awareness of the limitations of the last western emperors. Who is he? No emperor Lucius ever existed, but the Chronicle of Sigebert of Gembloux, which Geoffrey may well have known, gives Leo I a western colleague called Lucerius in the years 469-70. Sigebert is inaccurate here, having found the last series of ephemeral Augusti confusing, but the hint would have been sufficient, and Geoffrey was quite capable of turning "Lucerius" into the more familiar "Lucius."

We thus have both heads of the Empire, together fixing the main Gallic campaign in 469-70. Geoffrey also gives the name of a pope during Arthur's reign, Sulpicius. Tatlock explained this name as due to a garble, like the one that seems to explain Lucius. The pope whom Geoffrey read about somewhere, and may have remembered imperfectly, is Simplicius.[8] Simplicius's pontificate lasted from 468 to 483. Thus he was pope in the Leo-"Lucius" years. Geoffrey could have picked him up from the same chronicle of Sigebert that would have given him the emperors, though there is no need to insist on that particular source. The triple coincidence surely implies that in the Gallic episodes Geoffrey is using historical materials, more solid, perhaps, than the Welsh. His clues converge on the years 469-70. He knew something to indicate that Arthur, or a Briton whom he could take to be Arthur, campaigned in Gaul at that time.

Now we reach the crucial point. A Briton whom Geoffrey could have taken to be Arthur did campaign in Gaul at that time.

I noticed him nearly thirty years ago and came close to making the connection, but, alas, lost sight of him. More recently I looked again with some care. After realizing his significance I learned that others had glimpsed it too. Between 1138 and 1147, Sigebert's Chronicle, which I just mentioned, was expanded by a scribe at Ourscamp near Beauvais, who inserted a discussion of Geoffrey's work and came very near indeed to the essential insight. The English historian Sharon Turner, in 1799, attained it in a footnote though he backed away afterwards. The same issue was raised by Robert Huntington Fletcher in 1906, and has been raised again by Professor Gilbert Tournoy of Leuven. I am not speaking of some new-fangled personal fancy, but of a realization vastly senior to the "historical Arthur" hunt itself, which has diverted attention from it.[9]

The relevant events are as follows. In 467 Leo I appointed a western colleague, Anthemius. As soon as he could he initiated a short-lived attempt to retrieve the crumbling situation in Gaul. Several barbarian nations had occupied portions of the country. The Franks and Burgundians were fairly amenable, but troublesome Saxons had colonized the Loire valley as well as Britain, and the Visigoths, already entrenched in Spain, were threatening to advance from the south. With a view to checking the last-named, Anthemius negotiated a British alliance. In 468 a man described by the Gothic historian Jordanes as "the King of the Britons" crossed to Gaul, bringing, according to Jordanes, 12,000 troops.

One reason why his action has been overlooked or minimized by historians has been a notion that he was merely a chief of Bretons, that is, Britons who had migrated to Armorica and begun its transformation into Brittany. I think this is now agreed to be an impossible reading of the data. Even apart from plain testimony to his coming by sea, there were not yet enough Britons in Armorica to field an army with any prospect of checking the Visigoths, though the King may have recruited among them.10 He came from Britain, no doubt satisfied that counter-action had contained the Saxons in the island, and he probably made his way into Gaul via the Loire. About this time the Saxons along that river were dispersed in a battle near Angers, in which the King's Britons may have played a part.

But treachery was undermining him. Arvandus, Gaul's imperial prefect, approached the Visigoths with a proposal for them to crush the British army, then stationed on the Loire's north bank, and share out Gaul with the Burgundians. Arvandus was detected, but the Visigoths took up his idea. By then the King of the Britons had advanced to Bourges and turned south-westwards to meet them. No imperial support was forthcoming, and they defeated him in a hotly contested battle near Châteauroux. Probably early in 470 he took a remnant of his army into the nearby territory of the Burgundians, who had not joined in Arvandus's plotting and remained friendly. Here the record ends.

All this is attested by good evidence, some of it contemporary, not only in Jordanes but in Sidonius Apollinaris and Gregory of Tours; we have got away at last from the problems posed by enormous gaps of time. Geoffrey might conceivably have pieced it together from a careful reading of these three authors alone, possibly taking his first hint from Sigebert's Chronicle, which briefly mentions the British foray within a line or two of "Lucerius." But I find it easier to believe that he did have a lost source, even a "book in the British language," which assembled the scattered facts in a single narrative. Whether he did or not, it is clear that this episode provides a series of themes that can account for more of Geoffrey's story than the Welsh matter does.

The King of the Britons was in Gaul with his sea-borne army at the exact time defined by the chronological clues. He advanced to the neighbourhood of Burgundy. He was betrayed by a deputy-ruler conspiring with barbarians – that alien motif which Geoffrey imposes on Mordred. He fades from view after a fatal battle, with no recorded death. His continental career ends in Burgundy. All these things reappear in Geoffrey, however boldly (and characteristically) he has altered the details and circumstances. Indeed, as I remarked, the early prophecy of Arthur's demise which he ascribes to Merlin seems to imply that he first thought of it as happening in Gaul rather than Britain. Moreover, the King's apparent line of retreat at the end shows him moving towards the real Burgundian town of Avallon. Rachel Bromwich has observed, with no thought of the present topic, that Geoffrey's *Insula Avallonis* does not precisely Latinize the island's Welsh name *Avallach,* and that knowledge of the Burgundian town has influenced it.11

There are two immediate objections. The first is that Arthur fights the Romans, whereas for the King of the Britons they were allies, if equivocal and, in the end, worse than useless. The main answer is that Geoffrey changes the nature of the war as he changes the nature of other wars, for Arthur's glory.12 Arthur cannot rise to his apogee as a mere auxiliary. He must take on and vanquish the mightiest of opponents and, for a moment, reconstitute the Empire around himself. Actually, though, a tell-tale phrase is left embedded. When he is discussing his plans with a council, one of his sub-kings speaks of going to the continent to fight Romans *and Germans*. These "Germans" never appear; Geoffrey, presumably, took them from his source and forgot them; and in the source, the word could have referred to the real Germanic enemy, the Visigoths.

The second objection is the date given for Arthur's passing, 542. It conflicts with the entire chronological structure of the narrative which it brings to a close. Medieval texts are notoriously shaky on exact numerical dates, and 542 could be a mere scribal blunder. However, it is more interesting than that. Recognized processes of error could have produced it from the true date 470, the very year, probably, of the "passing" of the King of the Britons.

Before *Anno Domini* dating became the norm, some Christian writers used the chronology of Victorius of Aquitaine, devised in the fifth century, which counted from the year of Christ's passion. Victorius computed this as the year now called A.D. 28. In later times, copyists sometimes supposed dates on the Victorius scheme to be dates *Anno Domini*, and transcribed them with a 28-year error. That mistake is known to Arthurian texts: it happens twice in the *Historia Brittonum*. The Victorius equivalent of 470 would be 442. Geoffrey, or someone whose work he followed, could have found this given in a document as a date A.D. without being aware of the type of error involved. He could have recognized that 442 was unworkable for Arthur's demise, and, being determined to use the document at whatever cost, could have assumed a more familiar error of 100 years and mis-corrected the date to 542. (This very shift occurs in Wace's French paraphrase, where the error is increased by the conversion of 542 into 642.) Such a change would naturally have caused some upset, and, in confirmation, there are signs in Geoffrey's post-Arthur section of a confusion and an awkward re-thinking as to how much time elapsed between Arthur and the dispatch of Augustine's mission to Kent in 596. I will not go into that here, but will just observe that a primary source employing Victorius's dating, which dropped out of use in the sixth century, would have had to be a Latin one not too remote from the events and historically respectable. Geoffrey's hypothetical text in the British language might then have been the work of a Breton redactor who perpetrated the basic mistake.

Why has this King of the Britons been so little noticed before? Chiefly because he is referred to, with slight spelling variants, as Riothamus, and the assumption that this was his name has distracted attention from his Arthurian qualities. Professor Fleuriot, however, has shown that it Latinizes a style in the British language, *Rigotamos*. The first syllable means "king" and *tamo-* is a superlative suffix. "Riothamus" means "supreme king" or "supremely royal." In Welsh and Breton forms, it does become a name later as "Vortigern" does, but in the fifth century, like "Vortigern," it is almost certainly a title or honorific denoting a nominal high-kingship like Vortigern's. An analogous modern word is "generalissimo." There are many cases of such titles and honorifics being used to refer to powerful persons. "Genghis Khan," "Very Mighty Ruler," is a conspicuous instance. So is "Augustus," especially as meaning the first Roman emperor. Greek offers an exact etymological parallel to the British word, *Basileutatos,* and it was definitely not a name but a term of honour applied to Minos of Crete.[13]

Even if some new argument were to prove that the fifth-century "Riothamus" *was* the King's personal name, that would not rule out his having another, and since it is unlikely that his parents simply happened to give him a name so appropriate to the office he held as an adult, "Riothamus" would surely have been adoptive rather than baptismal and we are back to virtually the same conclusion. One way or another he was almost certainly called something else, and it is an open question what this was. A belief that it was "Arthur" (or Artorius), correct or not, can be inferred before Geoffrey. If we pursue the line of inquiry rejected by the "historical Arthur" school, and continue looking overseas, we come face to face with an intriguing document from Brittany. A. de la Borderie noted it in 1883, and so did E.K. Chambers in 1927, but it was ruled out as evidence by Tatlock in 1939, and subsequent scholars followed him without checking for themselves.

In 1019 the chaplain of the bishop of a Breton see produced a "life," or "legend," of St Gwyddno – in Breton, Gouéznou, and in the Latin of the existing manuscript, Goeznovius. The saint himself, one of many Welsh clerics who joined the British colonization of Armorica, has nothing to do with Arthur. But the *Legenda Sancti Goeznovii* has a preface with a chapter about the fifth-century events leading to their migration, and Arthur figures in it. Tatlock's denial of its independent value was grounded on his opinion – it was hardly more – that the date 1019 was spurious, and the author wrote much later and merely paraphrased Geoffrey. Fleuriot, however, has vindicated the date, and I have shown, myself, that the preface is not a précis of Geoffrey in any case and that the *Goeznovius* author is drawing on shared source-material farther back. He does in fact cite a prior work, which he calls the *Ystoria Britanica.*[14]

His fifth-century chapter is far too distant from the events to use directly as historical evidence, but it is free from manifest legend as the Welsh matter is not, and its account is so surprisingly good, in the light of present knowledge, that the implied underlying tradition deserves respect. The account introduces Arthur as Vortigern's successor, fighting Saxons in Britain as the Welsh assert, but also campaigning in Gaul (not against Romans; that is one of the reasons for rejecting the notion of copying from Geoffrey). It calls him the King of the Britons as Riothamus is called, and its historical sequence puts the Gallic warfare in or near the 460s. This author seems to be transmitting a continental tradition of Riothamus as the Britons' high king, making "Arthur" his personal name and associating him with warfare in Britain before his going overseas.15

Perhaps the solution of the Arthur problem is as simple as that. Perhaps "Arthur," or Artorius, was truly Riothamus's name and he appears under both styles, as a Spanish hero is sometimes Ruy Diaz de Bivar and sometimes El Cid Campeador. But "Arthur" might also have been a nickname or sobriquet, bestowed in his lifetime or, in some literary handling, later. One previous Artorius is on record in Britain, Lucius Artorius Castus, a Roman commander who took an army across the Channel in 184 to suppress an Armorican rebellion. If he was remembered (and there are reasons, if perhaps rather tenuous ones, for believing he was), a king taking another army across the Channel might have been hailed or commemorated as a "second Artorius." Another possibility looks almost comic, yet may be worth mentioning. The *h* in "Riothamus" is probably scribal; at the time, the Latin form would have been "Riotamus"; and "Artorius" is close to being an anagram of this. The letters RIOTAMUS can be arranged as they might have been, say, on a medallion, so as to suggest ARTORIUS, especially if we allow an added R for *rex*.16

Such speculations need not be insisted on. However, if we come down to chronicles compiled after Geoffrey's *History*, the clear persistence of a tradition allowing Arthur to be the same person as Riothamus is a weightier consideration. I already mentioned the Ourscamp copyist of Sigebert. My friend and colleague Professor Barbara Moorman has listed a whole series of passages pointing the same way, in Albericus Trium Fontium, the *Salzburg Annals*, Martinus Polonus, Jacques de Guise, Philippe de Vigneulles. The last speaks of dealings of Arthur with Aegidius, ruler of northern Gaul in the early 460s, for which Geoffrey gives no hint. Granted one or two minor and justified corrections – and I mean corrections, not emendations – all the allusions are consistent with a reign of Arthur extending from about 454 to 470. Strikingly, this is exactly where he is placed by the English chronicler Capgrave. Striking also is a Chronicle of Anjou which records Arthur's supposed career and refers to his betrayer as Morvandus – hard to explain unless we see it as a conflation of "Mordred" with "Arvandus," the name of Riothamus's actual betrayer, uncomprehendingly preserved.17

This is all in accord with my reluctance to ask directly "Did Arthur exist?" The nature of the question has altered. Riothamus, the high king, undoubtedly did exist. We even have a letter to him, by Sidonius. The question now is whether, under the name "Arthur" however acquired, he is the starting-point of the legend. I submit that we have good reason to think so. To state the issue another way, if the question "Did Arthur exist?" is pressed in that form, a defensible answer would be: "The Arthur of Geoffrey and the romancers is a legend, but he has a real original, the British high king who went to Gaul."

Arthur-Riothamus, as we might venture to call him, is the only documented person who does anything Arthurian. Wales offers no comparable evidence for a rival Arthur. Yet some of the matter which it does offer may well have a degree of validity. Can Arthur-Riothamus account for the Arthurian battles in the *Historia Brittonum*? Except by inference we know nothing of him in Britain before he took his army to Gaul. Was the resistance leader Ambrosius a general in his service, even a regent whose forces contained the Saxons during the royal absence abroad? Who can tell? But the *Goeznovius* preface indicates a belief that the King of the Britons did fight Saxons in Britain himself, before going to Gaul. If so, he could be the starting-point of the Welsh story as well as the continental one. Incidentally he would dispose of the claim – weak, but often urged – that Gildas's tract is an argument against Arthur because it does not mention him. Arthur-Riothamus would have flourished and left the scene long before Gildas's lifetime, and Gildas's knowledge of fifth-century individuals beyond the reach of his own memory is demonstrably so slight that silence means nothing. Bards may have been singing of the hero, but Gildas detested bards and would have taken no notice of what they said.

The Arthurian battle-list itself is thought to be based on a lost poem in Arthur's praise. It cannot be examined in detail here. Still, Arthur-Riothamus could have fought all the more-or-less locatable battles, which fit best into the context of the 450s and 60s. He has other features of geographical interest. His trans-Channel contact implies a domain in the West Country – Cornwall, Devon, Somerset, Dorset, the area which, when it emerges into history, forms a kingdom called Dumnonia. That same area offers the only reputed birthplace of Arthur, at Tintagel, and the only reputed grave, at Glastonbury. However fictitious the two stories may be, archaeology shows that they correspond to a relevant presence at about the right time. The Cadbury-Camelot hill-fort in Somerset, with its Arthurian lore and its unparalleled system of refortification, could have belonged to Arthur-Riothamus. He is in fact the only documented person who qualifies as the powerful, post-Roman royal refortifier whom archaeological findings suggest. But that topic likewise cannot be examined in detail here.[18]

One further point about this King of the Britons is the manner of his departure. He seems to vanish in Gaul, and there is no sign of a homecoming. The apparent reference in *Goeznovius* describes him as being "summoned from human activity," a phrase that need not imply immortality but may hint at disappearance rather than death. Here, surely, were the makings of the belief in an

Arthurian survival and destined return. The closest parallel to Arthur in this respect is the Portuguese legend of King Sebastian, and this arose from the fact that his death on a Moroccan campaign in 1578 was denied, with the result that after the Spanish annexation of Portugal his return as a national deliverer was fervently hoped for, and went on being hoped for long after any possible lifetime.

On the other hand I must stress that Arthur-Riothamus can hardly be the whole explanation, Arthur complete. Arthur's name is linked, if shakily, with the historical battle of Badon, and also with the "strife of Camlann" said to have occurred twenty-one years afterwards. In Geoffrey's hands they become battles at Bath and on the River Camel in Cornwall, fitted into Arthur's career before and during the reign of the emperor Leo, with no chronological scruples. But Gildas, writing when Badon was within living memory, puts it somewhere about 500, too late for Arthur-Riothamus. The *Annales Cambriae* put it later still, and Camlann, of course, later again, perhaps reflecting a tendency in some other Welsh matter to stretch Arthur far into the sixth century even while depicting him in terms inadmissible beyond the fifth.

I will not attempt a belated foray into these complications. What matters is that Arthur-Riothamus cannot cover all the early Arthurian data. What matters also, however, is that no single person could, because —as I said at the outset — the time-range is too wide. The same difficulty arises wherever in the range Arthur is put. It may be that the legendary King combines later figures with Arthur-Riothamus, so that he is a composite. That is the solution of a similar and worse problem with Merlin, who is compounded of two characters fully a century apart. But I have drawn attention to alternatives. For instance, a Welsh poem about a battle at a place called Llongborth refers to a force called "Arthur's Men" fighting in his absence and perhaps after his departure. Exploits ascribed by bards to Arthur's Men, on various occasions, could have inspired a notion that he was present in person when he was not, thereby extending his career. The Llongborth poem itself has been misconstrued in that sense, and so might others have been.[19]

These are topics for further consideration. What I am urging at the moment is that in the King of the Britons who went to Gaul we at last have an acceptable starting-point for the legend, a documented origin. After so many years of debate and dispute, that, surely, is progress.

Bibliography

Alcock, Leslie, (1) *Arthur's Britain*. London: Allen Lane, The Penguin Press, 1971. (2) "Cadbury-Camelot: a Fifteen-Year Perspective." *Proceedings of* the *British Academy* 68 (1982), pp. 355-88.

Annales Cambriae. See "Nennius."

Ashe, Geoffrey, (1) "A Certain Very Ancient Book." *Speculum* 56 (1981), pp. 301-23. (2) *The Discovery of King Arthur*. New York: Anchor Press, Doubleday, 1985, and Henry Holt, 1987. (3) *Kings and Queens of Early Britain*. London: Methuen, 1982.

Barker, Ernest, *From Alexander to Constantine*. London: Oxford, Clarendon Press, 1956.

Bromwich, Rachel, *Trioedd Ynys Prydein*. The Welsh Triads, with translation and notes. Cardiff: University of Wales Press, 1961.

Brown, Peter, *The World of Late Antiquity*. London. Thames and Hudson, 1971.

Campbell, James, ed., *The Anglo-Saxons*. Oxford: Phaidon, 1982; Ithaca, N.Y.: Cornell University Press, 1982.

Chambers, E.K., *Arthur of Britain*. London: Sidgwick and Jackson, 1927, reissue, 1966; New York: Barnes and Noble, 1964.

Day, Mildred Leake, ed., *Quondam et Futurus,* Summer 1987. Gardendale, Alabama.

Dumville, David, "Sub-Roman Britain: History and Legend." *History* 62 (1977), pp. 173-91.

Fletcher, Robert Huntington, *The Arthurian Material in the Chronicles*. Boston: Ginn, 1906; 2nd edition, New York: Franklin, 1966.

Fleuriot, Léon, *Les Origines de la Bretagne*. Paris: Payot, 1980.

Geoffrey of Monmouth, (1) *Historia Regum Britannie*. Edited by Neil Wright. Cambridge: D.S. Brewer, 1985. (2) *The History of the Kings of Britain*. Translated by Lewis Thorpe. Harmondsworth: Penguin, 1966.

Historia Brittonum. See "Nennius."

Lacy, Norris J., ed., *The Arthurian Encyclopedia*. New York: Garland, 1986.

Lapidge, Michael, and Dumville, David, eds., *Gildas: New Approaches*. Woodbridge: The Boydell Press, 1984.

Lietzmann, Hans, *From Constantine to Julian*. London: Lutterworth, 1953.

Loomis, Roger Sherman, ed., *Arthurian Literature in the Middle Ages*. Oxford: Clarendon Press, 1959; New York: Oxford, 1959. 2nd edition, 1961.

"Nennius." In *History from the Sources,* Vol. 8, *British History and the Welsh Annals*. Edited and translated by John Morris. Chichester: Phillimore, 1980.

Tatlock, J.S.P., (1) "The Dates of the Arthurian Saints' Legends." *Speculum* 14 (1939), pp. 345-65. (2) *The Legendary History of Britain*. Berkeley and Los Angeles: University of California Press, 1950.

Notes

[1] On the battles, see Leslie Alcock, *Arthur's Britain*, pp. 55-71; Geoffrey Ashe, *The Discovery of King Arthur* (hereafter cited as *Discovery*), pp. 67-73, 84-5, and arts. "Arthur, Origins of Legend," "Camlann," and "Nennius," in Norris J. Lacy, ed., *The Arthurian Encyclopedia* (hereafter cited as *Encyclopedia*). The German edition of *Discovery* is unsatisfactory and it should be consulted in English. For a destructive scrutiny of the Welsh records, see David Dumville, "Sub-Roman Britain: History and Legend," in *History* 62 (1977), pp. 173-91.

[2] Kenneth Jackson in R.S. Loomis, ed., *Arthurian Literature in the Middle Ages*, pp. 2-4.

[3] Jennifer Westwood made her observation in a BBC broadcast "Tuesday Call," on February 11th, 1986. E.K. Chambers, *Arthur of Britain*, pp. 221-7, gives a list of sleepers.

[4] Lewis Thorpe, trans., *The History of the Kings of Britain*, Introduction; Neil Wright, ed., *The Historia Regum Britannie of Geoffrey of Monmouth*, p. xvi.

[5] Ashe, "A Certain Very Ancient Book," in *Speculum* 56 (April 1981), pp. 301-23 (hereafter cited as *Speculum* 1981). Cp. Léon Fleuriot, *Les Origines de la Bretagne*, pp. 236-7, 245-7, 277, and Wright's edition of Geoffrey, pp. xvii-xviii.

[6] Ashe, *Discovery*, pp. 20-5, 47-8, 52. The classic discussion of the underlying mystique of the Empire, and the constant dream of regeneration, is in Ernest Barker, *From Alexander to Constantine*. See also Hans Lietzmann, *From Constantine to Julian*, and cp. Peter Brown, *The World of Late Antiquity*, p. 34.

[7] Ashe, *Discovery*, p. 89.

[8] J.S.P. Tatlock, *The Legendary History of Britain*, p. 251.

[9] Ashe, *Speculum* 1981, pp. 310-19 (primary source references for the ensuing discussion are given here), and *Discovery*, pp. 53-6, 96, 99-100. For Gilbert Tournoy, see Mildred Leake Day, ed., *Quondam et Futurus*, Summer 1987, pp. 6-8.

[10] Cp. James Campbell, ed., *The Anglo-Saxons*, p. 37, where it is suggested that this leader is credible as "a British ruler having authority on both sides of the Channel." Also Ian Wood in Michael Lapidge and David Dumville, eds., *Gildas: New Approaches*, pp. 21-2.

[11] Rachel Bromwich, *Trioedd Ynys Prydein*, pp. 267-8. "Avallon" is Gaulish and is derived from a word meaning "apple," as the name of the island is generally taken to be, certainly by Geoffrey.

[12] In his account of the third-century revolt of Carausius in Britain and the Roman reconquest, he turns one of the Romans' successful commanders, Asclepiodotus, into a British king fighting against them. Thus Asclepiodotus's victory becomes a British triumph and a Roman defeat.

[13] Plutarch, *Life of Theseus*, 16. The significant relationship between *Rigotamos* and cognate British "high king" designations is discussed in Ashe, arts. "Riothamus" and "Vortimer" in *Encyclopedia*.

[14] Chambers, *Arthur of Britain*, pp. 92-4, 241-3; Tatlock, "The Dates of the Arthurian Saints' Legends," in *Speculum* 14 (1939), pp. 361-5; Fleuriot, *Les Origines de la Bretagne*, p. 277; Ashe, *Speculum* 1981, pp. 304-6. Cp. Wright's edition of Geoffrey, p. xvii.

[15] Ashe, *Discovery*, pp. 102-6, and art. *"Goeznovius"* in *Encyclopedia*.

[16] Jackson in Loomis, ed., *Arthurian Literature in the Middle Ages*, p. 2; Fleuriot, *Les Origines de la Bretagne*, pp. 47-8; Ashe, *Kings and Queens of Early Britain*, pp. 42-3, 132-3. Lucius Artorius Castus is linked with Arthurian origins by advocates of what is known as the Sarmatian Connection. See Helmut Nickel, art. "Arms and Armor" in *Encyclopedia*. The emperor Domitian was reviled by Christians and others as a "second Nero," and a figurative use

of "Nero" as the emperor's name by Juvenal becomes, in Geoffrey of Monmouth, a literal one. As for anagrams, "Voltaire," the celebrated *nom de plume* of François Marie Arouet, is said to have been an anagrammatic formation.

17 Ashe, *Discovery*, pp. 106-11; Fleuriot, *Les Origines de la Bretagne*, p. 118.

18 Ashe, *Discovery*, pp. 70-2, 117-8, and art. "Cadbury-Camelot" in *Encyclopedia*; Alcock, "Cadbury-Camelot: a Fifteen-Year Perspective," in *Proceedings of the British Academy* 68 (1982), pp. 358, 362-8, 380-5.

19 Jackson in Loomis, ed., *Arthurian Literature in the Middle Ages*, p. 13; Ashe, *Discovery*, pp. 121-3.

Medieval French Arthurian Literature: Recent Progress and Critical Trends

By KEITH BUSBY, *Universities of Utrecht and Leiden*

✠

The specialist of medieval French literature enjoys a privileged position. Historical circumstances during the twelfth and thirteenth centuries in particular, which I do not need to go into in detail here, led to the position of French as the seminal vernacular literature in Europe for most of the Middle Ages. With the notable exceptions of the epic, which seems to be a universal phenomenon, and the lyric, which appears first in Provençal, the first examples of most genres in the vernacular are in French; most types of medieval vernacular literature are imported from French-speaking regions into other countries where they are translated, and more usually, adapted. The outline of the dissemination of French literature in the rest of Europe is well-known and so I shall not repeat it here. Only with the rise of Italian in the fourteenth century does French literature begin to lose its monopoly, although this only amounts to its relegation to a shared first place, not to a displacement as such.

It therefore follows logically – fortunately for the scholar of French – that some knowledge of Old French language and literature is a pre-requisite for germanists, netherlandists, scandinavists, anglicists, catalanists, occitanists, hispanists, lusitanists, italianists, even celticists. The existence of Czech and Serbian version of the *Tristan* is witness to the penetration eastwards of medieval French literature, and to the west there are versions of a number of French texts in Middle Irish. In the south, many translations and adaptations from the French have been preserved in the Iberian peninsula, and to the north, Iceland seems to have acquired the taste for French literature early in the thirteenth century.[1] This gallicization of European literature in the Middle Ages is demonstrable, as I have just suggested, simply by virtue of the existence of translations and adaptations of actual Old French works. Yet French influence goes even deeper than this, for more significantly perhaps, genres, themes, motifs, styles, and modes that find their first expression in French are also absorbed into other literatures.

It is important to underline here that we are not usually confronted with literal translations from French into, say, English or Old Norse, or slavish imitations in these languages of established French genres. Certainly, these exist, but they are the exception rather than the rule. What makes the comparative study of medieval European literature so interesting is the way in which French texts are adapted to meet the needs of new audiences, and the ways in which indigenous productions ingeniously transform French models into something characteristic of their own time and place. Staying within the theme of this colloquium, it is enough to recall how different Hartmann von Aue's *Iwein* and *Erec* are from Chrétien de Troyes's originals, and how brilliantly different Wolfram von Eschenbach's *Parzival* is from Chrétien's own Grail romance; the Middle English *Ywain and Gawain* and *Sir Percyvelle of Galles* are typically English romances, but both composed with a first-hand knowledge of Chrétien; and from Scandinavia, it is fascinating to see how the authors of *Erexsaga*, *Percevalssaga / Valverspattr*, and *Tristramssaga* adapt French romances to meet the requirements of the native saga tradition. On the other hand, we have works such as the Middle English *Sir Gawain and the Green Knight*, the Middle High German *Diu Crône* by Heinrich von dem Türlin, the Middle Dutch *Walewein* – to quote but three –, all undoubted masterpieces not modelled on specific French originals, yet showing a profound knowledge of French tradition, remoulded by their respective indigenous conventions.

If this sounds like a *pro domo* plea, then it is, but its real purpose in the present context is to stress the fact that French Arthurian literature stands at the beginning of the Arthurian literary tradition in whatever language and whatever period. Clearly, I do not here mean Celtic origins, as interesting as they are, nor the transformation of the historical or legendary Arthur up to and including Wace. Both of these topics are outside of my competence and can best be left to others more qualified than myself. The Arthurian literature I shall consider begins with the first romance proper, Chrétien de Troyes's *Erec et Enide*. A distinction should, of course, be made between conventional critical use of the term *romance*, and the use in Old French of the word *romanz*. By *romance*, I mean the kind of purely fictional courtly narrative in which all but conventional claims to historicity have disappeared. Without stirring up the hornet's nest of genre-definitions, and what a romance is precisely, it is at least evident that when Wace calls his *brut* a *romanz*, he uses the word in its primary sense of "a translation into the romance vernacular from Latin," in his case, Geoffrey of Monmouth's *Historia Regum Brittaniae*. Whilst it is also undoubtedly "courtlified" to a certain extent, it is not an Arthurian romance in the sense that we now generally understand the term, mainly because Chrétien de Troyes is the founder of the genre.

Normally, one would hesitate to claim that one particular poet founded a genre, but research shows that it is in many respects true in the case of Chrétien de Troyes and Arthurian romance. There are precedents for many features of Chrétien's romances, stylistic and material, in earlier Frech and Latin literature, but there is nothing prior to him that can properly be compared with *Erec et Enide*, *Cligés*, *Lancelot*, *Yvain*, or *Perceval*. We are often taught at university that medieval authors did not invent their works *ex nihilo* because the Middle Ages did not prize originality. This often proves a stumbling-block for students who have learned elsewhere to attach a premium to novelty. The truth is, of course, that we often present it in the wrong terms: the Middle Ages *did* appreciate originality, but it was of a different kind, and as for invention, the Latin rhetorical term *inventio* is the one that comes closest to encapsulating the medieval poet's art. An *inventor* is a *trouvère*, a *troubadour*, someone who is skilled at *finding* his material and applying his skill to it. Chrétien's *inventio* transforms whatever Arthurian and other material he had at his disposal into something profoundly original and radically experimental. It is this that justifies considering Chrétien de Troyes as the initiator and founder of Arthurian romance.

Chrétien's presence in medieval French literature, even outside of Arthurian romance, is so strong that his legacy has to be reckoned with a good deal of the time. A large part of French romance can be seen to develop in reaction to Chrétien, and in view of the irradiation of French literature in the rest of Europe, his *oeuvre* assumes a central place in Arthurian literary studies as a whole. From the French standpoint, Chrétien creates the episodic verse romance practised by himself and his epigones; he introduces into French (and world) literature the Grail theme, which would alone have assured him lasting fame; the popularity of his works also played a considerable part in the genesis of the Vulgate Cycle and the later prose romances, such as the *Tristan* and *Guiron le Courtois*. It is, I think, important to be aware of the place of Chrétien in the evolution of Arthurian literature not merely because without him it would have been quite different, but also because the study of French Arthurian literature, which is my concern here, is in many ways Chrétien-centred.[2]

If one accepts, as one must, the fact that without Chrétien there would have been no Hartmann or Wolfram, without the Vulgate Cycle and the prose *Tristan*, no Malory, then it can be reasonably claimed that we need to understand the nature of the one in order properly to appreciate the genesis and particularities of the others. Hartmann knew why Chrétien wrote as he did and recognised what he had to modify in order to please his own audience; Malory understood the principle of *entrelacement* in the Old French prose romances so well that he was able to unlace them to meet the requirements of his own narrative structures. These two examples are quoted solely by way of illustration and as an indication of my hope that the orientation that follows in recent French Arthurian scholarship may also be of help to those who study what might be called – without any condescension – the legacy of French Arthurian literature.

II

The history of Arthurian scholarship would provide enough material for several *thèses d'états*, and so what follows only pretends to be a brief analytic survey of the present state of our knowledge. Neither does it make any claims to being exhaustive; the steady growth in the number of items in the annual *Bulletin Bibliographique de la Société Internationale Arthurienne (Bibliographical Bulletin of the International Arthurian Society)* renders that out of the question. The existence of this invaluable publication has, however, made my task a good deal easier, and I hereby acknowledge the frequent use made of it. What I have tried to do is to point to some of the major achievements in French Arthurian scholarship[3] of the last quarter of a century, and to discern some of the basic directions in which critics have been, and still are, moving. I shall also indicate what seem to me obvious *lacunae* and *desiderata* in the field.

The choice of a period of some twenty-five years (1962-87) is to some extent arbitrary and will only be used as a rough practical delimination. The sixties, however, do seem to me the decade in which the study of French Arthurian romance came of age, as it were, along with other fields of medieval scholarship. This is not to cast any derogatory aspersions on pre-sixties scholarship with the arrogance of hindsight; anyone who has as much as flirted with Arthurian literature will realise the vast amount of work done by earlier scholars and will be irresistibly reminded of Bernard of Chartres's well-known comment about dwarves standing on the shoulders of giants. Yet the sixties do seem to constitute a watershed during which certain kinds of criticism peter out and others become established. It is in order to provide a context for the body of this paper that I therefore begin with a brief look at the major concerns of earlier French Arthurian scholarship.

Two convenient landmarks which reveal contemporary concerns – at an interval of approximately thirty years – are James Douglas Bruce's *The Evolution of Arthurian Romance From the Beginnings Down to the Year 1300* (2 vols., 1923, revised in 1928 by Alfons Hilka) and Roger Sherman Loomis's now dated but still invaluable compendium, *Arthurian Literature in the Middle Ages* (1959).[4] Bruce's work represents a summation of Arthurian scholarship up to the beginning of the 1920's, and is concerned mainly, but not exclusively, with French literature. *Evolution* is a key-word, reflecting as it does the early twentieth-century desire to trace lines of development across the whole corpus of Arthurian romance. Some of the chapter headings will give an indication of where the accents lie: "Early Traditions concerning Arthur"; "Origins of the Lays and Romances"; "Chrétien, Robert de Boron, and the Theory of Christian Origin"; "The Theory of Celtic Origin"; "Beginnings of the Prose Romances"; "Development of the Vulgate Cycle"; "The Influence of the Prose Romances on subsequent Literature"; "Supplementary Observations on the Question: Were there Arthurian Romances before Chrétien?"; "The Mabinogion Controversy"; "Miss Weston's Gawain-Complex"; "Robert de Boron, his Origin, the Date of his Poem, and its Relation to the Didot-Perceval." Origins, beginnings, development, influence, dating: these matters are what Arthurian scholarship was largely about in Bruce's day. In a sense this was inevitable, for many texts had not long been edited, and Arthurian studies, whilst not quite in their infancy, were just beginning to gather steam. Most of the work was done on Chrétien on the one hand and on the Grail romances on the other; the post-Chrétien verse romances and much of the corpus of prose romance, notably the prose *Lancelot* and the prose *Tristan*, were relatively neglected.

Whilst Bruce's monumental work is fairly representative and reasonable synthesis of trends current at the time, Loomis's compendium (*ALMA*), consisting of forty-one essays by twenty-nine scholars in an attempt to cover Arthurian literature in all languages, is at one and the same time a more diversified and a much more engaged book. In that its authors are among the most distinguished scholars of the time, and in that they refrain by and large from presenting solely their own point of view, *ALMA* does typify Arthurian scholarship in the late sixties, but one proviso must be made. Loomis was a man with pronounced views on Arthurian literature and the most vociferous proponent of the theory of Celtic origins. This partly determined his choice of contributors and of topics covered, for in addition to essays on most major authors and works, there are pieces on "The Oral Diffusion of the Arthurian Legend" and "The Origin of the Grail Legends" by Loomis himself, and on "The Origin and Growth of the Tristan Legend" by his pupil, Helaine Newstead. Moreover, it is known that Loomis occasionally indulged in what might today be called "creative editing" on some of the other chapters, apparently without consulting their authors.[5] In his concern with Celtic origins, Loomis carries on an earlier fashion, but develops the methods in a much more sophisticated manner than his predecessors. Another of his major publications, *Arthurian Tradition and Chrétien de Troyes* (1949) is a detailed demonstration of how Welsh and Irish analogues can be found for practically every episode and motif in Chrétien's works.[6] Many other earlier interests were also pursued in the period between Bruce and Loomis, and these are reflected in *ALMA*: chronology, interrelationships between various Grail romances, and so on. Two main features, however, distinguish synchronic views of French Arthurian studies taken in the early twenties and in the late fifties. The first of these is a slight but discernible tendency to expand the canon of texts studied, as testified in particular by the essays on the Chrétien epigones ("Miscellaneous French Romances in Verse") by Alexandre Micha, on the Vulgate Cycle by Jean Frappier, and on the prose *Tristan* by Eugène Vinaver. Frappier and Vinaver in particular came to dominate French Arthurian scholarship through much of the fifties and sixties, and their work also embodies the second of the two features characteristic of the later period. Roughly put, that is the attention paid to French Arthurian romances as literary works of art, where the subjects of investigation are structure, style, and meaning, rather than origins and influences.[7]

Some examples of frequently studied issues will illustrate this point. There is in early work on Chrétien little attention paid to the narrative structure of his romances, whereas the fifties and early sixties in particular produced a plethora of articles devoted to the bipartite or tripartite structure of *Erec et Enide* or *Yvain* or *Lancelot*.[8] The structure of the episodic romances was also contrasted with that of the prose cycles with the development (but not discovery) by Vinaver of the principle of *entrelacement*. Much work also concerned with the dominant concepts of courtly love, chivalry, and religion as portrayed in the romances. Some of this was related to analysis of the motivation of characters, in a manner that some scholars now regard as being somewhat alien to the nature of romance. Whether that is true or not, the sixties sees a decline in the number of articles that suggest why Erec treats Enide so harshly, or why Arthur does not seem too concerned about Guenièvre's affair with Lancelot in *La Mort le roi Artu*. The same is true of the kind of structural analysis mentioned above, although investigation into the architectonic principles of the prose romances is still making up lost time. Why precisely these kinds of issues concern scholars less from the mid-sixties onwards is difficult to say; some would cynically claim that there is simply a limit to the number of interpretations that can be put on Gauvain's behaviour in *Yvain* or *Perceval* and that Chrétien's narratives are capable of illustrating only a restricted number of patterns. It is perhaps fairer to conclude that the kind of studies that characterize contemporary scholarship proceed more or less logically from earlier work and that the process is another illustration of a standard form of scholarly progress.[9]

III

With regard to modern achievement, the easiest thing to measure, of course, is the appearance of good scholarly editions of texts that improve on previous ones. There have been five notable recent editions of post-Chrétien episodic verse romances: of *Durmart le Gallois* by Joseph Gildea (2 vols., 1965-66), of *Le Roman de Silence* by Lewis Thorpe (1972 [an *editio princeps*]), of *Fergus* by Wilson Frescoln (1983), of *Yder* by Alison Adams (1983), and of *Hunbaut* by Margaret Winters (1984). Critical response to these tends to suggest that they will remain the standard editions for many years, with the exception of Frescoln's *Fergus,* which has come in for a good deal of criticism. R.C. Johnston and D.D.R. Owen also edited the two short Gauvain texts, *Le Chevalier à l'Epée* and *La Mule sans Frein* (1972). A number of short Arthurian texts have also been re-edited by P.M.O'H. Tobin, in *Les lais anonymes des XIIe et XIIIe siècles* (1976). Grail literature has been particularly fortunate in that William Roach has now completed his masterly edition of the Continuations of Chrétien's *Perceval*; in addition to the three redactions of the First Continuation (1949-55), Roach has published the Second Continuation (1971) and the Continuation of Manessier (1983). These exemplary editions will put study of the important corpus of Continuations on a much sounder footing, but the study still needs to be encouraged.[10] Roach's pupil, Lenora D. Wolfgang, has also produced a definitive edition of the *Bliocadran,* one of the pseudo-prologues to *Perceval* (1976).

The achievement of Roach's Continuations is matched by work in the field of prose romance. Most of the prose *Tristan* is now available, thanks to partial editions by Joël Blanchard (1976) and the three-volume edition of Carpentras 404 by Renée L. Curtis (1963, 1976, 1985). Unfortunately, as the Carpentras manuscript is incomplete, the final part of this text still awaits a proper edition. For three-quarters of a century, scholars had to make do with H.O. Sommer's uncritical transcription of a single manuscript of the prose *Lancelot* (vols. III-V of his seven-volume edition of the Vulgate Cycle, 1908-16). We now have what almost amounts to an *embarras de richesses* with Alexandre Micha's nine-volume edition of the cyclical version of the romance (1978-83) and Elspeth Kennedy's non-cyclical version in two volumes (1980). Neither of these are liable to be superseded, as both are the fruits of decades of close acquaintance with the manuscripts. Other prose texts that have appeared in excellent editions are the *Folie Lancelot*, a portion of the *Suite du Merlin*, edited by Fanni Bogdanow (1965), the prose version of Robert de Boron's *Merlin* by Alexandre Micha (1980), and the complete prose version of Robert's trilogy edited from the Modena manuscript by Bernard Cerquiglini (1981). The first and fourth parts of the enormous fourteenth-century *Perceforest* have been edited for the first time by, respectively, Jane Taylor (1979) and Gilles Roussineau (2 vols., 1987). Oddly enough, perhaps, the most urgent desideratum in French Arthurian literature are properly critical editions of the romances of Chrétien de Troyes to replace the composite series of Foerster / Hilka and the uncritical and sometimes inaccurate CEMA texts of Roques / Micha / Lecoy.[11]

Accompanying these new editions are a number of indispensable reference works. The *Arthurian Encyclopedia* (1986) is a handy and reliable source of information on aspects of the field with which one may not be especially well-acquainted. In the bibliographical sphere, there is the general, but unfortunately often inaccurate and incomplete *Arthurian Bibliography* by C.E. Pickford and R.W. Last (2 vols., 1981-83, with supplement, 1986), and Edmund Reiss, Louise Horner Reiss and Beverly Taylor, *Arthurian Legend and Literature: an Annotated Bibliography*, vol. 1: The Middle Ages (1984). On specifically French topics, there is Douglas Kelly's bibliography of Chrétien de Troyes (1976, supplement in preparation), and David Shirt's bibliographical guide to the *Tristan* poems (1980); if Marie de France can be considered a writer of Arthurian poems, then mention must be made of Glyn S. Burgess's bibliography (1977, Supplement No. 1, 1986). Research has also been greatly facilitated by G.D. West's two remarkable onomastic works, on French verse romance (1969), and on French prose romances (1978). For Chrétien specialists, Marie-Louise Ollier's *Lexique et concordance de Chrétien de Troyes* (1986) will be a constant companion, although one regrets that it had to be based on the Guiot copy of Chrétien's romances. For *Perceval*, this should be used in conjunction with Gabriel Andrieu and Jacques Piolle's concordance of that romance (1976). Andrieu, Piolle and May Plouzeau have also produced a similar concordance of Béroul (1974), whilst Pierre Kunstmann and Martin Dube have generated a concordance of *La Mort le roi Artu* (1982).[12]

These editions and reference works correspond to a continuing vitality of the more critical side of French Arthurian studies, which in turn frequently reflects concerns and tendencies visible in literary scholarship as a whole and medieval literary scholarship in particular. It is thus possible to discern in recent work on French Arthurian literature articles and books which make use on the one hand of such general approaches as reception theory, intertextuality, psychoanalysis, structuralist narratology, deconstruction, and feminism, and on the other of more specifically period-orientated concerns such as the importance of patronage, audiences, and the social background in general, rhetorical poetics and the relationship to Latin literature, patristic exegesis, the relationship of romance to the folktale, and a growing awareness of the importance of the role played by scribes and the compilers of manuscripts.

Arguably, the most obvious difference between French Arthurian studies now and a quarter of a century ago is what might be termed the expansion of the canon. Research into Chrétien de Troyes properly goes on unabated, but those works now generally known as the epigonal romances – the verse texts written in the wake of Chrétien – have benefited from a considerable revival of interest.[13] Some of this is due to the recent editions of a number of romances mentioned above, but the most influential force is doubtless the seminal study of Beate Schmolke-Hasselmann, *Der arthurische Versroman von Chrestien bis Froissart* (1980), which effectively rewrites a part of medieval literary history. Among the many merits of this book are its consideration of the meaning of *Epigonentum* for Arthurian romance and re-assessment of the epigonal romances in terms other than those of odious comparison with Chrétien. Authors are seen to react consciously and with particular purposes to the models they found in Chrétien, and their productions are not regarded as pale and degraded imitations of the master. This view of the corpus of French Arthurian verse romance stresses both the continuity of Chrétien's presence and the evolution of the genre to meet changing cultural and social conditions. A similar approach is taken in my own thematic study of Gauvain (1980), which also examines the prose romances up to 1225, and the two-volume collaborative *The Legacy of Chrétien de Troyes* (1987-88) edited by Norris J. Lacy, Douglas Kelly, and myself. It is now at last possible to speak of a *Receptionsgeschichte* of Chrétien's *oeuvre,* although a good deal more remains to be done. A similar re-appraisal of the "nachklassiche Aventiureroman" is observable in German literary studies; particularly important is Christoph Cormeau's study of *Wigalois* and *Diu Crône* (1977).

Schmolke-Hasselmann's work also lays considerable emphasis on the question of intended publics, both specifically in terms of patrons, and generally in terms of larger primary audiences. One can clearly see here the influence of Hans Robert Jauss's audience-oriented work on genres and in particular of Erich Köhler's crucial *Ideal und Wirklichkeit in der höfischen Epik,* which as early as 1956 offered a socio-historical explanation of the genesis of French Arthurian romance. Schmolke-Hasselmann affirms the possibility that *Erec et Enide* was written to commemorate the investiture of Henry II's third son, Geoffrey, as Duke of Brittany. Further, she plausibly suggests that Guillaume le Clerc's *Fergus* was written for the northern English Balliol family; Girard d'Amiens's dedication of *Escanor* to Edward I and Eleanor of Castille is another case in point. Both of these romances reflect English claims to the throne of Scotland, and even the writing of Froissart's *Meliador* (before 1383) is bound up with Edward III's problems north of the border. Generally speaking, French Arthurian verse romance reflects the interests, frequently family and territorial, of the Anglo-Angevin nobility of the twelfth and thirteenth centuries, who constitute its primary audience. Schmolke-Hasselmann has also devoted an important article to the role of the literary Round Table as a driving-force in British politics of the time (1982). We are therefore justified in considering much French Arthurian romance as English literature in French rather than French literature. The consequences of this proposition have yet to be fully assimilated, especially as it is liable to be true of other forms of non-Arthurian narrative of the time.[14]

It is no less true to speak of a revival in the fortunes of the Old French prose romances in the last two decades, and the healthier state of editions is matched by an increase in the number of studies devoted to them. This area, benefitting from the earlier work of Eugène Vinaver in particular, has been dominated recently by Fanni Bogdanow, Emmanuèle Baumgartner, Elspeth Kennedy and Alexandre Micha. In many respects, study of the prose romances was less advanced than that of Chrétien, and much more basic work has had to be done here. Elspeth Kennedy and Alexandre Micha have both occupied themselves extensively with the prose *Lancelot*, and their editing has led in critical work to considerable emphasis being laid on the part played by copyists and compilers in the evolution of prose romance. Micha has examined the manuscript tradition of the *Lancelot* in a series of meticulous studies, and Kennedy has shown scribes at work in a number of articles. The latter's study of the *Lancelot and the Grail* (1986) is an essential accompaniment to her edition, and Micha has also announced a volume of *Essais sur le cycle du Lancelot-Graal*. His general *Etude sur le 'Merlin' de Robert de Boron* (1980) should likewise accompany a reading of his edition of the text mentioned above. A pupil of Vinaver, Fanni Bogdanow applies many of his observations about the elaboration of prose romances – that is to say the manner in which these texts come gradually into being by a process of cumulation of material and re-adjustment – to what she calls the Post-Vulgate *Roman du Graal*. We still await Dr. Bogdanow's edition of this text. Baumgartner's essential thesis on the prose *Tristan* (1975) brings for the first time clarity to the problem of the various redactions of the work, and looks at the romance from most points of view – structural, thematic, etc. The same author's later work stresses the way in which Biblical history is re-written and used as a structure for some of the prose romances, particularly the *Estoire del Saint Graal* and the Vulgate *Queste*.[15] Many of the findings of the above scholars have been applied to the Vulgate cycle by E. Jane Burns in her study of the Vulgate Cycle (1985), where Zumthor's work on *mouvance* is also employed. This book rejects the application of aesthetic criteria alien to the thirteenth century, laying emphasis on the fluidity of the prose romance tradition and on the constant re-writing effected by the tale itself, "li contes." Mention should also be made here of Colette-Anne van Coolput's excellent study of the reception of the *Queste* in the various versions of the prose *Tristan*, in many ways another "state of the art" book.[16]

No critical study of Arthurian romance, of course, is written in isolation, and most will reflect tendencies visible elsewhere. Most of those mentioned above, however, have concerned themselves with specifically Arthurian problems and in some ways constitute directions of their own. Jane Burns's book on the Vulgate cycle, as I have mentioned, owes a good deal to Paul Zumthor, and it is worthwhile looking briefly at the concept of *mouvance* in particular and its implications for Arthurian studies.[17] The fundamental instability of the medieval text leads to its "moving" freely in space and time, to the creation of various redactions and *remaniements*, all of which are at the same time autonomous and fragments of a larger whole. The prose romances, which almost without exception show considerable textual divergences from one manuscript to another, are particularly susceptible of explanation in terms of *mouvance*, thereby avoiding the invidious search for the "original", the "earliest", or the "best" version. *Mouvance* is an inestimable help in studies of the prose romances, and it could also be used to good avail in long overdue studies of the Continuations of Chrétien's *Perceval,* The different versions of some *chansons de geste* might also be explicable in this manner, but it ought not to be imagined that it is a universal panacea, which is what some of its proponents seem to claim. The status of the text of a prose romance is very different from that of a romance by Chrétien de Troyes, where the authorial presence and the constraints of metre and rhyme allow *mouvance* to operate only on a micro-level. This brings us back ultimately to the question of text editions: *mouvance* could be used to justify logically the CFMA editions of Chrétien, in practice a *reductio ad absurdum* of non-interventionist editing, and tantamount to denying the historical existence of poet, Chrétien de Troyes, who once chose every single word with the utmost of care.[18]

Related to *mouvance* is another concept that medievalists have very evidently found to correspond to a basic critical need, that of *intertextuality*. Developed largely by Michael Riffaterre in connection with post-medieval literature, the idea has been modified somewhat to fit the particularities of the medieval situation, and is now currently employed by a large number of scholars, foremost among whom is Karl D. Uitti. What used to be rather randomly attributed to the "influence" of one text on another or an "allusion" in one text to another is now seen as a constitutive feature of the medieval intertext, according to which one text owes its identity, in part at least, to its intertextual relationships to others. The well-known links between Chrétien's *Yvain* and *Lancelot*, for example, seen intertextually, appear as purposefully evocative and provocative, causing the medieval listener to regard the two romances as part of a larger whole. Chrétien's use of the *Tristan* romances takes the process a stage further, outside of his own work and into the wider field of courtly narrative, and so on. When later authors seem to allude to Chrétien or make use of material they found in his romances, the intertextuality is intended not just to place their own work in a tradition, but also to invite detailed comparison between their work and his. It is thus not difficult to see how intertextual analyses would be possible of, say, the rewriting of Chrétien's *Charrette* episode in the prose *Lancelot*, or of the transformations of the grail theme from Chrétien's *Perceval* right through to passages of the prose *Tristan*.

If medieval writing and rewriting can be seen from an intertextual point of view, they can also be viewed, as I hinted in my remarks on Chrétien's originality towards the beginning of this paper, as a rhetorical process subject to the "rules" and prescriptions of the medieval arts of poetry. The scholar who has done the most to increase our understanding of this aspect of medieval literature is Douglas Kelly, and fortunately for Arthurian studies, much of Kelly's work has been on Chrétien and the prose cycles. Early work on the relevance of the Latin arts of poetry to vernacular literature tended to be limited to the demonstration of the presence of, say, *amplificatio* or *abbreviatio*, in a given work, or showing, for example, that a female portrait was in confirmity with the prescription found in Geoffrey of Vinsauf's *Poetria Nova*. A deeper understanding of how medieval poets set to work suggests that invention (*inventio*) is the most important procedure. Invention is the finding, the identification, of the material (*materia*) as suitable for treatment in the literary work. The *materia remota* is the source material, and the *materia propinqua*, the changes and adaptation the author applies to it. The invention of material operates on various levels, from a purely stylistic one (the choice of words) through the identification of suitable ornamental devices to that of the narrative itself (the *fabula*). All this is of clear relevance to Chrétien's own aesthetic as it is found in his prologues (and the key terms of *san*, *matiere*, and *conjointure*) and as it can be distilled from his works in general.[19] Prose romances are seen to employ what Kelly calls *disjointure* rather than *conjointure*: the constant rewriting, interpolation, and readjustment noted early on by Vinaver and analysed in terms of *mouvance* by Jane Burns is seen by Kelly as a particular form of invention, consisting both of the identification of new material as suitable and of the adaptation of existing material to fit the new. The linking of Biblical and legendary Arthurian material in the Vulgate cycle is an example. The art of the prose romance is thus not so much one of accumulation but of absorption.

The obvious relevance of Latin rhetorical works for the understanding of Old French literature raises the more general issue of the relationship between vernacular literature and Latin works circulating at the time. Despite this being a self-evident field for investigation, it has not received the attention it deserves in French Arthurian studies. The need for such work has been eloquently restated by Tony Hunt in an important article on "Chrestien and the *Comediae*," which shows the indebtedness of certain dramatic aspects of Chrétien's work to these Latin poems. Given the position of Latin literature throughout the whole Middle Ages, and the fact that many vernacular writers must have been educated in the schools and brought up on a mainly Latin curriculum (about which we are not entirely uninformed), this is unlikely to be an isolated case. One other notable, if not uncontroversial, contribution to this area of Arthurian studies is Claude Luttrell's *The Creation of the First Arthurian Romance* (1974), an attempt, amongst other things, to show the influence on Chrétien of Alanus de Insulis. If Luttrell is correct, a revision of our traditional dating of Chrétien is called for. Neither the proposed redating nor the thesis in general have been universally accepted, but Luttrell's work and the scholarly debate it inspired, largely between himself and Tony Hunt, indicates that much remains to be done in this area.[20] A re-examination of the relationship of French Arthurian romance, and Old French literature in general, to medieval Latin is another of my urgent *desiderata*.

Growing awareness of the importance of rhetoric for our understanding of the way in which medieval authors composed their works has been to some extent matched by attempts to ascertain how medieval audiences reacted to them. A medieval audience may not have thought of the poet's art as *inventio*, but it would certainly have appreciated the choice and treatment of material; a primary audience would certainly have understood any socio-historical implications of the romances such as Schmolke-Hasselmann has discerned them; and most medieval audiences – depending, of course, on their level of knowledge – would have appreciated the intertextual game authors were often playing with them. The question of how much medieval audiences actually knew is absolutely crucial in any attempt to reconstruct their *Erwartungshorizont* and subsequent reaction. Beate Schmolke-Hasselmann has described the primary audience of French Arthurian verse romance as consisting of expert enthusiasts capable of recognising the subtle quotations and allusions of which the texts are full. If this at least is plausible – after all, there would be no point in referring to other parts of the tradition if the audience could not be expected to grasp the point – another approach to medieval literature, the exegetical-allegorical method, has not won general acceptance. The method was first applied with success to Middle English literature, especially to Chaucer, by D.W. Robertson, Jr. in his *A Preface to Chaucer* (1962). Effectively, the method involves reading all medieval literature using the techniques with which medieval people learned to read the Bible. This means interpretation, passing through the stages of *Littera, sensus* and *sententia*, until the deeper meaning (which has to be related to to the Augustinian concepts of *caritas* and *cupiditas*) is revealed.[21] Whilst the relevance of this to such romances as the Vulgate *Queste* or *Estoire* may be justified, it is not easy at first sight to see what application it might have to, say, Chrétien de Troyes. Nevertheless, attempts are not lacking, notably those by Jacques Ribard (1972), who proposes seeing Chrétien's *Lancelot* as an allegory of salvation, and Tom Artin, whose *The Allegory of Adventure* (1974) attempts something similar with *Erec et Enide* and *Yvain*. If the method and theory are not inherently implausible – and some kinds of literature even seem to require them – the most serious obstacle to their acceptance in Arthurian studies seems to be that of the theological knowledgeability of the audiences of the twelfth and thirteenth centuries. It may be plausible to assume that Chrétien knew his St. Augustine and other patristic writings, but it is probably not so to assume the same for his audience. As far as one can judge, the vogue of the Robertsonian method has made scholars more aware of, say, the messianic associations of the

Lancelot-figure, although it is no longer practised as such. Like most methods and approaches with some degree of plausibility, it has bequeathed some of its most useful tools to the common arsenal of medieval literary scholarship.

A scholar of the fifties returning to French Arthurian literary studies after an absence of two decades or more, catching up on the work carried out in the interim, would probably be struck by the fact that Arthurian romance seems to appear more humourous in the eyes of his colleagues. Whilst it had been recognised that Chrétien showed intermittent flashes of humour, the first major work to propose a consistently ironic interpretation of Arthurian romances is Peter Haidu's *Aesthetic Distance in Chrétien de Troyes* (1968). According to Haidu, Chrétien creates distance between his audience and his characters, enabling the former to stand back and evaluate the latter's behaviour critically and ironically. One of the most important devices Chrétien uses is dramatic irony, for example, establishing parallels between two scenes and thereby inviting comparison, or giving the audience more information than the characters, thus leading to humour. During the same period, D.D.R. Owen also suggested in an important article, published in 1970, that Chrétien had specifically parodic and burlesque intentions in *Cligés* and *Lancelot*. A major study by the Germanist D.H. Green, *Irony in Medieval Romance* (1979), is also concerned with Chrétien; its conclusions are susceptible of wide application. With regard to later romance, I might cite certain pages of my study of Gauvain (1980), and a number of sections in Beate Schmolke-Hasselmann's book, particularly those devoted to *Fergus*, *Meraugis de Portlesguez*, and *La Vengeance Raguidel*, where humour is seen to be often dependent on the relationship of the later texts to Chrétien. Prose romances have by and large not been interpreted in this manner, and it is probably true that they do not lend themselves as well to it; an obvious exception, of course, is the treatment in the prose *Tristan* of the figure of Dinadan. The net result of the "ironic" stream of criticism is that we are nowadays much more sensitive to possible humour in Arthurian romance; the danger, of course, is that of not knowing where to draw the line, for what appears to us as comic may have seemed deadly serious to a medieval audience. Medieval humour is a subject that requires serious investigation.

When I suggested earlier that scholars no longer really seem concerned whether Chrétien's romances are bipartite or tripartite in structure, I did not mean to suggest that narrative structure is no longer a topic of current interest. On the contrary, it remains centre-stage, but in different guises to those it assumed earlier. Recent work on the prose romances mentioned above has moved away from looking at narrative structure as a static phenomenon, and tends to concentrate either on the unfolding of the tale as the principle of narrative structure (Burns) or on the act of invention (Kelly). Structural analysis of verse romance lays more emphasis on the typology of the narrative, on how the conventions and patterns that constitute the structure of romance are first of all established by Chrétien and later adapted by his epigones. This is again evident from Schmolke-Hasselmann's book and an excellent article of hers on the typology of the romance opening.[22]

Matilda Bruckner (1980) has analysed in detail the different manifestations of the convention of hospitality in a small corpus of Arthurian and non-Arthurian works from the end of the thirteenth century. Significantly, Bruckner applies to medieval romance the methods of Russian formalism, structuralism, and semiotics, and shows how the work of, say, Claude Lévi-Strauss on myths, Roland Barthes, Claude Bremond, and Julia Kristeva on more literary narrative, can be used to discern convention and innovation in romance structures. A number of other scholars, too numerous to mention here, have also produced important work in what may generally be considered a structuralist / semiotic perspective, clearly deriving from the general field of "narratology" developed by theoreticians such as those mentioned above and others, notably A.-J. Greimas and Tzvetan Todorov. Medievalists who take this line tend to be younger American scholars intent on demonstrating that medieval literature, usually neglected by theoreticians, is susceptible of analysis in the same way as the modern narrative canon. Predictably, perhaps, most of this type of work has been in connection with Chrétien, and prose romance has on the whole not yet been examined in this way. Special mention should be made of Donald Maddox's study of *Erec et Enide, Structure and Sacring* (1978), a pioneering work seen by its author as a contribution to the development of an anthropology of medieval narrative. The most evident danger in such scholarship – and some have not been slow to point this out – is that the desire to test the validity of the model chosen leads to neglect of the text itself as a unique and autonomous work of art. It seems to me doubtful whether the particular recent interest in "deconstruction" is liable to prove as fruitful when applied to Arthurian romance as the Greimasian strain, but Peter Haidu, whose more recent work also has a strongly semiotic tendency, has made a first attempt in a recent article on *Yvain* (1983).

The application of structuralist narratology to medieval Arthurian romance appears to be an American phenomenon. Another clearly discernible recent movement in medieval studies, which also reflects developments in theory and post-medieval literature, that of psychoanalytical readings, seems a largely Francophone phenomenon. Freud has, oddly enough, not been much used, despite obvious potential, but Freud is not very much in fashion these days. Two articles from 1967 and 1968 by Jean Györy on Chrétien's imagery are more Jungian than Freudian, and the more recent work of Charles Méla and Roger Dragonetti, despite the inclusion of some of it in the series "Connexions du Champ freudien", seems to owe more to the late editor of the series, Jacques

Lacan, than to Freud, Dragonetti's study of Chrétien's *Perceval, La vie de la lettre au moyen âge* in particular, whilst arguably in an etymological tradition that goes back at least as far as Isidore of Seville, has been criticised for being based on subjective and random word-association. Méla's study of the corpus of Grail romances, *La reine et le Graal* (1984), is altogether a much more substantial piece, showing the importance of such themes as castration and incest, implicit and explicit, in the Grail romances. Positivistic scholars are almost certain to regard his work, like that of Dragonetti, as ultimately subjective and personal.

The psychoanalytical approach is, of course, ultimately anthropological in that it deals with universals and mental, social and cultural patterns inherent in the human psyche. Other French work shows the same kind of tendencies. The studies of Pierre Gallais, one of the most individualistic of the French critics, is eclectic and wide-ranging. Gallais's first two books have a distinct orientalist bent, using the work of Henri Corbin and proposing Iranian analogies for Chrétien's *Perceval* (1972) and specific sources for the *Tristan* (1974). In a sense, these two books are an orientalist counterbalance to the Celtic "sourcisme" of Roger Sherman Loomis and Jean Marx current in the fifties and early sixties. Gallais's third book, *Dialectique du récit médiéval* (1982) combines the application of Greimasian narratology with an approach derived from the work of cultural anthopologists such as Gilbert Durand and Robert Blanché. In this work, the narrative structures of Chrétien de Troyes's romances are shown to embody basic hexagonal and spiral patterns. Gilbert Durand's *Structure anthropologiques de l'imaginaire* also forms the point of departure for another recent book on Chrétien, this time concentrating on his symbolism, by Gallais's pupil, Gérard Chandès (1986). More traditional structural kinship anthropology has been applied, also largely to Chrétien, in a number of articles by Jean-Guy Gouttebroze.

Some of this narratological and anthropological work makes frequent reference to the work of the Russian folklorist, Vladimir Propp, and the nature of romance in general invites comparison with the popular tale. In the field of Arthurian romance, this has been carried out once more in connection with Chrétien (and Marie de France insofar as she can be considered Arthurian). With the exception of Edgar Sienaert's book on Marie (1978), the folkloric approach is again a peculiarly French phenomenon. Whilst similarities between Arthurian romance and the folktale have always been recognised, early work did little more than catalogue analogues and common motifs. This stage is now behind us, and the emphasis in recent contributions by Edina Bozóky (1978), Jean-Charles Payen (1978), and in particular an important article by Anita Guerreau (1983), is on the transformation of folkloric material to meet the different requirements of courtly literature.

Finally, it is hardly surprising to note that studies of French Arthurian romance have not been unaffected by the recent rise of feminism, and a multitude of articles have appeared investigating in particular the role of women in romance. However, it is disappointing to note that most of these are descriptive rather than critical, and fail to address what is probably the most interesting issue of Arthurian romance from a feminist point of view, that is to say, to what extent the nature and spirit of the genre are determined by gender-specific elements in both authors and audiences. Some pertinent remarks, however, are to be found in articles by Roberta L. Krueger (1983 and 1985), the second of which is part of a special issue of *Romance Notes* devoted to the topic of *Courtly Ideology and Woman's Place in Medieval French Literature*, which concludes with a full bibliography on the subject, to which those interested are referred for further details.

It will, I hope, be clear from this lengthy but incomplete survey of recent scholarship on medieval French Arthurian literature that the field is in a healthy and vital state. The various critical tendencies I have tried to discern show that Arthurian literature not only provides its own specific problems but that it is equally open and receptive to critical fashions and movements developing elsewhere in connection with both medieval and post-medieval literature.[23] Generally speaking, recent progress is visible in three main areas: firstly, what I have termed an expansion of the canon, which is leading us towards a much fuller picture of Arthurian romance as it appeared to medieval audiences; secondly, a growing awareness of the importance of audience response, and of various aspects of both primary and secondary reception; thirdly, a growing sophistication in the selection and application of methods of analysis.

There are nevertheless serious *lacunae* and urgent *desiderata*: the ones that concern me most as a specialist in Old French literature are the lack of critical editions of Chrétien de Troyes, the failure of scholars to avail themselves of William Roach's editions of the Continuations of *Perceval* and seriously tackle these extremely important texts, and the lack of investigation of the Latin background to vernacular literature. Other fields that would certainly prove fruitful require close examination of manuscripts: the relationship between text and illumination in the illustrated manuscripts, what the manuscript context of romances can tell us about the way they were read, etc. Not many medievalists to-day dirty their hands in manuscript rooms, the deceptive lure of the handy CFMA, TLF or SATF edition being too strong. The manuscripts of Arthurian romance constitute one of our few real points of contact with medieval reality and we cannot risk losing it. Developments in new critical methodology seem to be in many safe pairs of hands, whilst those who work with primary manuscript material (in whatever way) are dwindling in number. Faithful conference-attenders may have noted that in the recent past the *antiqui* and the *moderni* have been digging in on opposite sides of a critical no-man's land. Allow me to conclude this paper, which has on the whole been optimistic about the state of Old French Arthurian scholarship, with a plea for a *rapprochement* between the philologists and the theoreticians. Any analysis of a medieval text or texts, however abstract, requires a sound philological base, and philologists and positivistic scholars need to re-examine and re-adjust their critical positions so as to avoid falling back into a vicious circle of repetition and banality.[24] I propose that we meet here again in Odense in the year 2010 to see whether this wish has been met and to examine further progress brought about by the vitality of the Arthurian legend.

Bibliographical Appendix

This appendix contains details of all works specifically mentioned in the text of the article, and other books and articles representative of authors or tendencies. The divisions largely follow the order in which subjects are discussed in the article. The choice of items discussed in the article and listed here is a personal one, although I feel it is reasonably representative. Those interested in following up the work of a particular scholar or critical approach are referred in the first instance to the subject and author index of the annual *Bulletin Bibliographique de la Société Internationale Arthurienne* (*Bibliographical Bulletin of the International Arthurian Society*), and further to the other bibliographies listed below.

Earlier Arthurian Scholarship

Bruce, James Douglas, *The Evolution of Arthurian Romance From the Beginnings Down to the Year 1300*. Göttingen: Vandenhoeck und Ruprecht, 1923, 2 vols. 2nd edition with bibliographical supplement by Alfons Hilka, Göttingen: Vandenhoeck und Ruprecht, 1928.

Loomis, Roger Sherman, ed. *Arthurian Literature in the Middle Ages. A Collaborative History*. Oxford: Clarendon Press, 1959.

-- --. *Arthurian Tradition and Chrétien de Troyes*. New York: Columbia Univ. Press, 1949.

Recent Text Editions

Durmart le Galois, roman arthurien du treizième siècle. Ed. Joseph Gildea. Villanova, PA.: Villanova Univ. Press, 1965-66, 2 vols.

Le Roman de Silence, a Thirteenth-Century Arthurian Verse-Romance by Heldris de Cornuälle. Ed. Lewis Thorpe. Cambridge: Heffer, 1972.

Guillaume le Clerc, *The Romance of Fergus*. Ed. Wilson Frescoln. Philadelphia: W.H. Allen, 1983.

The Romance of Yder. Ed. and tr. Alison Adams. Woodbridge: Boydell and Brewer, 1983.

The Romance of Hunbaut, an Arthurian Poem of the Thirteenth Century. Ed. Margaret Winters. Leiden: Brill, 1984.

Two Old French Gauvain Romances: 'Le Chevalier à l'Epée' and 'La Mule sans Frein. Eds. R.C. Johnston and D.D.R. Owen. Edinburgh / London: Scottish Academic Press, 1972.

Les lais anonymes des XIIe et XIIIe siècles. Ed. Prudence Mary O'Hara Tobin. Geneva: Droz, 1976.

The Continuations of the Old French 'Perceval' of Chrétien de Troyes. Ed. William Roach. Philadelphia: Univ. of Pennsylvania Press / The American Philosophical Society, 1949-83. 5 vols. Vol. I: The First Continuation, Redaction of MSS. *TVD*, Univ. of Pennsylvania Press, 1949; rpt. The American Philosophical Society, 1965.

Vol. II: The First Continuation, Redaction of MSS. *EMQU*, Univ. of Pennsylvania Press, 1950; rpt. The American Philosophical Society, 1965.

Vol. III. pt. i: The First Continuation, Redaction of MSS. *ALPRS*, The American Philosophical Society, 1952. rpt. 1970.

Vol. III, pt. ii: Glossary of the First Continuation, by Lucien Foulet, The American Philosophical Society, 1955.

Vol. IV: The Second Continuation, The American Philosophical Society, 1971.

Vol. V: The Continuation of Manessier, The American Philosophical Society, 1983.

Bliocadran, a Prologue to the *Perceval* of Chrétien de Troyes. Ed. Lenora D. Wolfgang. Tübingen: Niemeyer, 1976.

Le roman de Tristan en prose. Les deux captivités de Tristan. Ed. Joël Blanchard. Paris: Klincksieck, 1976.

Le roman de Tristan en prose. Ed. Renée L. Curtis. Munich: Fink, 1963; Leiden: Brill, 1976; Woodbridge: Boydell and Brewer, 1985. 3 vols.

Lancelot, roman en prose du XIIIe siècle. Ed. Alexandre Micha. Geneva: Droz, 1978-83. 9 vols.

Lancelot do Lac, the Non-Cyclic Old French Prose Romance. Ed. Elspeth Kennedy. Oxford: Clarendon Press, 1980. 2 vols.

La Folie Lancelot a Hitherto Unidentified Portion of the *Suite du Merlin* Contained in MSS B.N. fr. 112 and 12599. Ed. Fanni Bogdanow. Tübingen: Niemeyer, 1965.

Robert de Boron. *Merlin*, roman du XIIIe siècle. Ed. Alexandre Micha. Geneva: Droz, 1980.

Robert de Boron. *Le roman du Graal.* Ed. Bernard Cerquiglini. Paris: 10/18, 1981.

Le roman de Perceforest, première partie. Ed. Jane H.M. Taylor. Geneva:

Droz, 1979.

Le roman de Perceforest, quatrième partie. Ed. Gilles Roussineau. Geneva: Droz, 1987. 2 vols.

Reference Works

The Arthurian Encyclopedia. Ed. Norris J. Lacy et al. New York: Garland, 1986.

Pickford, C.E., and R.W. Last.*The Arthurian Bibliography*. Woodbridge: Boydell and Brewer, 1981-83. 2 vols. Supplement, 1986.

Reiss, Edmund, Louise Horner Reiss, and Beverly Taylor. *Arthurian Legend and Literature: an Annotated Bibliography*, vol I: The Middle Ages. New York: Garland, 1984.

Kelly, Douglas. *Chrétien de Troyes: an Analytic Bibliography*. London: Grant and Cutler, 1976.

Shirt, David J. *The Old French Tristan Poems: a Bibliographical Guide*. London: Grant and Cutler, 1980.

Burgess, Glyn S. *Marie de France: an Analytical Bibliography*. London: Grant and Cutler, 1977. Supplement no. 1, 1986.

West, G.D. *An Index of Proper Names in French Arthurian Verse Romances (1150-1300)*. Toronto: Toronto Univ. Press, 1969.

-- --. *An Index of Proper Names in French Arthurian Prose Romances*. Toronto: Toronto Univ. Press, 1978.

Ollier, Marie-Louise. *Lexique et concordance de Chrétien de Troyes*. Montreal: Institut d'études médiévales / Paris: Vrin, 1986.

Andrieu, Gabriel, and Jacques Piolle. *Concordancier complet des formes graphiques occurrentes du 'Perceval' de Chrétien de Troyes*. Aix-en-Provence: CUER MA, 1976.

-- --, -- --, and May Plouzeau. *Le roman de 'Tristan' de Béroul: concordancier complet des formes graphiques occurrentes*. Aix-en-Provence: CUER MA, 1974.

Dube, Martin, and Pierre Kunstmann. *Concordance analytique de la 'Mort le roi Artu'*. Ottawa: Editions de l'Univ. d'Ottawa, 1982.

The Expansion of the Canon: Verse Romance

Schmolke-Hasselmann, Beate. *Der arthurische Versroman von Chrestien bis Froissart: zur Geschichte einer Gattung*. Tübingen: Niemeyer, 1980.

Busby, Keith. *Gauvain in Old French Literature*. Amsterdam: Rodopi, 1980.

-- --, Douglas Kelly, and Norris J. Lacy. *The Legacy of Chrétien de Troyes*.Amsterdam: Rodopi, 1987-88. 2 vols.

Cormeau, Christoph. *'Wigalois' und 'Diu Crône': zwei Kapitel zur Gattungsgeschichte des nahklassischen Aventiureromans*. Munich: Artemis, 1977.

The Historical and Legal Background
Schmolke-Hasselmann, Beate. "The Round Table: Ideal, Fiction, Reality." *Arthurian Literature*, 2 (1982), 41-75.
Bloch, R. Howard. *Medieval French Literature and Law*. Berkeley / Los Angeles / London: Univ. of California Press, 1977.
Shirt, David. J. "Chrétien de Troyes et une coutume anglaise." *Romania*, 94 (1973), 178-95.
-- --. "*Cligés*: a Twelfth-Century Matrimonial Case-Book?" *Forum for Modern Language Studies*, 18 (1982), 75-89.

The Expansion of the Canon: Prose Romance
Kennedy, Elspeth. *Lancelot and the Grail: a Study of the Prose 'Lancelot'*. Oxford: Clarendon Press, 1986.
-- --. "The Scribe as Editor." *Mélanges ... Jean Frappier*. Geneva: Droz, 1970. Vol. I, pp. 521-31.
Micha, Alexandre. "Les manuscrits du *Lancelot en prose*." *Romania*, 81 (1960), 145-87; *ibid.*, 84 (1963), 28-60 and 478-99.
-- --. "La tradition manuscrite du *Lancelot en prose*." *Romania*, 85 (1964), 293-318 and 478-517; *ibid.*, 86 (1965), 330-59.
-- --. *Etude sur le 'Merlin' de Robert de Boron*. Geneva: Droz, 1980.
Bogdanow, Fanni. *The Romance of the Grail: a Study of the Structure and Genesis of a Thirteenth-Century Arthurian Prose Romance*. Manchester: Manchester Univ. Press, 1966.
Baumgartner, Emmanuèle. *Le 'Tristan en prose': essai d'interprétation d'un roman médiéval*. Geneva: Droz, 1975.
-- --. *L'arbre et le pain: essai sur la 'Queste del Saint Graal'*. Paris: SEDES, 1981.
Burns, E. Jane. *Arthurian Fictions: Rereading the Vulgate Cycle*. Columbus, OH.: Miami Univ. Press, 1985.
Van Coolput, Colette-Anne. *Aventures querant et le sens du monde: aspects de la réception productive des premiers romans du Graal cycliques dans le 'Tristan en prose'*. Louvain: Louvain Univ. Press, 1986.
Dembowski, Peter F. *Jean Froissart and his 'Meliador': Context, Craft and Sense*. Lexington, KY.: French Forum, 1983.
Taylor, Jane H.M. "The Fourteenth Century." In *The Legacy of Chrétien de Troyes*, vol. I, pp. 267-332.

Mouvance and Intertextuality
Zumthor, Paul. "Intertextualité et mouvance." *Littérature*, 41 (February 1981), 8-16.
Uitti, Karl D. *Story, Myth and Celebration in Old French Narrative Poetry 1050-1200*. Princeton: Princeton Univ. Press, 1973.

-- --. "Narrative and Commentary: Chrétien's Devious Narrator in *Yvain*." *Romance Philology*, 33 (1979-80), 160-67.
-- --. "Intertextuality in *Le chevalier au lion*." *Dalhousie French Studies*, 2 (1980), 3-13.
Dembowski, Peter F. "Intertextualité et critique des textes." *Littérature*, 41 (February 1981), 17-29.
Krueger, Roberta L. "Reading the *Yvain* / *Charrete*: Chrétien's Inscribed Audiences at Noauz and Pesme Aventure." *Forum for Modern Language Studies* 19 (1983), 172-87.
Bruckner, Matilda Tomaryn. "Intertextuality." In *The Legacy of Chrétien de Troyes,* vol. I, pp. 223-65.

Rhetoric and the Latin Background
Kelly, Douglas. "Topical Invention in Medieval French Literature." In *Medieval Eloquence: Studies in the Theory and Practice of Medieval Rhetoric.* Ed. James J. Murphy. Berkeley / Los Angeles / London: Univ. of California Press, 1978, pp. 231-51.
-- --. "Obscurity and Memory: Sources for Invention in Medieval French Literature." In *Vernacular Poetics in the Middle Ages.* Ed. Lois Ebin. Kalamazoo, MI.: Medieval Institute Publications, 1984, pp. 33-56.
-- --. "L'invention dans les romans en prose." In *The Craft of Fiction: Essays in Medieval Poetics.* Ed. Leigh A. Arrathoon. Rochester, MI.: Solaris Press, 1984, pp. 119-42.
Hunt, Tony. "The Rhetorical Background to the Arthurian Prologue." *Forum for Modern Language Studies*, 6 (1970), 1-23.
-- --. "The Prologue to Chrestien's *Li contes del graal*." *Romania*, 92 (1971), 359-79.
-- --. "Tradition and Originality in the Prologues of Chrestien de Troyes." *Forum for Modern Language Studies*, 8 (1972), 32-44.
-- --. "Chrestien and the *Comediae*." *Medieval Studies*, 40 (1978), 120-56.
Luttrell, Claude. *The Creation of the First Arthurian Romance: a Quest.* London: Edward Arnold, 1974.

Patristic Exegesis
Ribard, Jacques. *Chrétien de Troyes: le 'Chevalier de la Charrette', essai d'interprétation symbolique.* Paris: Nizet, 1972.
Artin, Tom. *The Allegory of Adventure: Reading Chrétien's 'Erec et Enide' and 'Yvain'.* Lewisburg / London: Bucknell Univ. Press, 1974.

Humour and Irony

Haidu, Peter. *Aesthetic Distance in Chrétien de Troyes: Irony and Comedy in 'Cligés' and 'Perceval'*. Geneva: Droz, 1968.

Owen, D.D.R. "Profanity and its Purpose in Chrétien's *Cligés* and *Lancelot*. *Forum for Modern Language Studies*, 6 (1970), 37-48.

Green, D.H. *Irony in Medieval Romance*. Cambridge: Cambridge Univ. Press, 1979.

Busby, Keith. "The Likes of Dinadan: the Role of the Misfit in Arthurian Literature." *Neophilologus*, 67 (1983), 161-74.

Narrative Structure

Schmolke-Hasselmann, Beate. "Untersuchungen zur Typik des arthurischen Romananfangs." *Germanisch-Romanische Monatsschrift*, NS 31 (1981), 1-13.

Bruckner, Matilda Tomaryn. *Narrative Invention in Twelfth-Century French Romance: the Convention of Hospitality (1160-1200)*. Lexington, KY.: French Forum, 1980.

Maddox, Donald L. *Structure and Sacring: the Systematic Kingdom in Chrétien's 'Erec et Enide'*. Lexington, KY.: French Forum, 1978.

Haidu, Peter. "Repetition: Modern Reflections on Medieval Aesthetics." *Modern Language Notes,* 92 (1977), 875-87.

-- --. "Romance: Idealistic Genre or Historical Text?" In *The Craft of Fiction: Essays in Medieval Poetics*. Ed. Leigh A. Arrathoon. Rochester, MI.: Solaris Press, 1984, pp. 1-46.

-- --. "The Hermit's Pottage: Deconstruction and History in *Yvain*." *Romanic Review*, 74 (1983), 1-15.

Psychoanalysis

Györy, Jean. "Prolégomènes à une imagerie de Chrétien de Troyes," *Cahiers de Civilisation Médiévale*, 10 (1967), 361-84, and 11 (1968), 29-39.

Dragonetti, Roger. *La vie de la lettre au moyen âge (le conte du Graal)*. Paris: Seuil, 1980.

Méla, Charles. *Blanchefleur et le saint homme ou la semblance des reliques*. Paris: Seuil, 1979.

-- --. *La reine et le Graal. La Conjointure dans les romans de Graal, de Chrétien de Troyes au 'Livre de Lancelot'*. Paris: Seuil, 1984.

Cultural and Structural Anthropology

Gallais, Pierre. *Perceval et l'initiation*. Paris: Editions du Sirac, 1972.

-- --. *Genèse du roman occidental. Essais sur 'Tristan et Iseut' et son modèle persan*. Paris: Tête de Feuilles / Sirac, 1974.

-- --. *Dialectique du récit médiéval (Chrétien de Troyes et l'hexagone logique)*. Amsterdam: Rodopi, 1982.

Chandès, Gérard. *Le serpent, la femme et l'épée. Recherches sur l'imagination symbolique d'un romancier médiéval: Chrétien de Troyes*. Amsterdam: Rodopi, 1986.

Gouttebroze, Jean-Guy. "L'arrière-plan psychique et mythique de l'itinéraire de Perceval dans le *Conte du Graal* de Chrétien de Troyes." In *Voyage, quête, pélerinage* (*Senefiance*, 2). Aix-en-Provence. CUER MA, 1976, pp. 341-52.

-- --. "Cousin, cousine. Dévolution du pouvoir et sexualité dans le *Conte du Graal*." In *Chrétien de Troyes et le Graal*. Paris: Nizet, 1984, pp. 77-87.

Arthurian Romance and Folktale

Sienaert, Edgar. *Les Lais de Marie de France: du conte merveilleux à la nouvelle psychologique*. Paris: Champion, 1978).

Bozóky, Edina. "Roman arthurien et conte populaire: les règles de conduite et le héros élu." *Cahiers de Civilisaton Médiévale*, 21 (1978), 31-36.

Payen, Jean-Charles. "L'enracinement folklorique du roman arthurien." *Mélanges ... Jean Rychner* (*Travaux de linguistique et de littérature*, 16, 1 [1978]), pp. 427-439.

Guerreau, Anita. "Romans de Chrétien de Troyes et contes folkloriques. Rapprochements et observations de méthode." *Romania*, 104 (1983), 1-48.

Feminism

Burns, E. Jane, and Roberta L. Krueger, eds. *Courtly Ideology and Woman's Place in Medieval French Literature*. Special issue of *Romance Notes*, 25, 3 (Spring 1985).

-- --, and -- --. Introduction. *Ibid.*, 205-19.

Krueger, Roberta L. "Love, Honor, and the Exchange of Women in *Yvain:* Some Remarks on the Female Reader." *Ibid.*, 302-17.

-- --. "Loyalty and Betrayal: Iseut and Brangien in the *Tristan* Romances of Béroul and Thomas." In *Sisterhood Surveyed: Proceedings of the Mid-Atlantic Women's Studies Association, 1982 Conference*. Ed. Anne Dzamba Sessa. West Chester, PA.: West Chester Univ., 1983, pp. 72-78.

Notes

[1] I shall not document this part of the paper, but refer those interested to the bibliographies listed in the appropriate section of the bibliographical appendix

[2] On Chrétien as founder of the genre and his legacy, see Norris J. Lacy, Douglas Kelly, and

Keith Busby (eds.), *The Legacy of Chrétien de Troyes*, 2 vols. (Amsterdam: Rodopi, 1987-88).

³ For the sake of clarity, let me make clear that when I say "French Arthurian scholarship" I mean "scholarship on French Arthurian literature."

⁴ Full references to all works mentioned in the course of this paper can be found in the appropriate section of the bibliographical appendix.

⁵ This remark is, frankly, based on hearsay, but from what I consider to be a reliable source.

⁶ On Loomis, see Claude Luttrell, "The Arthurian Traditionalist's Approach to the Composer of Romance: R.S. Loomis on Chrétien de Troyes," *Oeuvres et critiques*, 5, 2 (Winter 1980-81), 23-30. This issue of *Oeuvres et critiques* is of general interest here, as it is devoted entirely to the subject *Réception critique de l'oeuvre de Chrétien de Troyes*.

⁷ On Frappier and Vinaver, see s. v. in *The Arthurian Encyclopedia*, eds. Norris J. Lacy et al. (New York: Garland, 1986), and on Frappier, Jean-Charles Payen, "Une approche classiciste du roman médiéval: Jean Frappier, lecteur de Chrétien de Troyes," *Oeuvres et critiques*, 5, 2 (Winter 1980-81), 45-52.

⁸ See, for a modern evalutation of these divisions, Donald L. Maddox, "Trois sur deux: théories de bipartition et de tripartition dans les oeuvres de Chrétien," *Oeuvres et critiques*, 5, 2 (Winter 1980-81), 91-102; also Rosemarie Jones, "Chrétien devant la critique anglaise contemporaine: questions de structure," *ibid.*, 15-22.

⁹ A good idea of scholarly concerns during a particular period can be gotten from leafing through a few numbers of the International Arthurian Society's bibliographical bulletin mentioned above.

¹⁰ See my review article on Roach's project and critical response to it, in *Romance Philology*, 41, 3 (February 1988), 298-309.

¹¹ A group of British scholars have made a start on this; I am myself editing *Perceval*. See, on the problems of Chrétien editions, T.B.W. Reid, "Chrétien de Troyes and the Scribe Guiot," *Medium Aevum*, 45 (1976), 1-19, and the article by Tony Hunt referred to in note 18 below.

¹² The use of computers in the humanities opens up all kinds of possibilities for medieval studies of which we have only begun to scratch the surface.

¹³ They would not now be referred to as "Miscellaneous French Romances in Verse," the title Micha gave to his *ALMA* chapter. It is to be regretted that the same author's contribution to the new *Grundriss der romanischen Literaturen des Mittelalters*, IV/1 (Heidelberg: Winter, 1978), pp. 377-99, does little more than reproduce the *ALMA* chapter.

¹⁴ It is also worthwhile pointing out that the legal background of Arthurian romance has received some attention recently, particularly from David Shirt and R. Howard Bloch, whose work shows how romance reflects real legal concerns of the time. Full references are in the bibliographical appendix.

¹⁵ This is quite a different matter to the mere tracing of biblical and doctrinal sources in, say, the *Queste*, which is the case for Pauline Matarasso's rather turgid *The Redemption of Chivalry* (Geneva: Droz, 1979).

¹⁶ The expansion of the canon also seems to be a chronological one. Both Peter F. Dembowski and Jane H.M. Taylor have recently published important work on fourteenth-century romances, such as Froissart's *Meliador, Perceforest, Isaie le Triste*.

¹⁷ The classic description of *mouvance* is to be found in Zumthor's *Essai de poétique médiévale* (Paris: Seuil, 1972), pp. 65 ff.

¹⁸ See especially Tony Hunt, "Chrestien de Troyes: the Textual Problem", *French Studies*, 33 (1979), 257-71.

¹⁹ One of the by-products, as it were, of the renewed interest in rhetoric is the number of

recent articles devoted to the prologues of medieval romance, in particular those of Chrétien. See especially the articles by Tony Hunt listed in the section on rhetoric and the Latin background in the appendix.

[20] See the exchange in *Bulletin Bibliographique de la Société Internationale Arthurienne*, 30 (1978), 209-37, and 32 (1980), 250-75.

[21] For a convenient guide to the issues involved, see the articles by E. Talbot Donaldson, R.E. Kaske, and Charles Donahue in *Critical Approaches to Medieval Literature: Selected English Institute Papers, 1958-59,* ed. Dorothy Bethurum (New York / London: Columbia Univ. Press, 1960).

[22] This means the opening of the narrative proper, not the prologue.

[23] Cf. Stephen G. Nichols, Jr., "Deeper into History," *L'Esprit Créateur,* 23, 1 (Spring 1983), 91-102, p. 91: "Medieval French studies do not suffer, as they once did, from a lack of openness to new critical methodologies."

[24] One hopeful sign is that medievalists are at least beginning to articulate their concern for the fate of their discipline. See in particular Paul Zumthor, *Parler du moyen âge* (Paris: Minuit, 1980), and a special number of *L'Esprit Créateur,* 23, 1 (Spring 1983), devoted to *The Future of Medieval French Studies.*

Middle English Arthurian Romance: The Repetition and Reputation of Gawain

By PHILLIP C. BOARDMAN, *University of Nevada*

✠

There are close to 120 romances in Middle English (not counting those in Chaucer and Gower). Of these some thirty are Arthurian – more than one fourth. These range in length from extensive reworkings of the French Vulgate like Lovelich's *Merlin* at nearly 28,000 lines down to ballads of a few hundred lines. Some versions are in alliterative verse, others are in couplets or in tail-rime stanzas, and, of course, Malory's cycle is in prose. While most are anonymous, one is by the greatest Middle English poet, Chaucer. While many exist in several versions and manuscripts, some survive to us miraculously in single copies.

The study of a chronological list of the earliest Arthurian romances traces a movement from France and then Germany in the twelfth and early thirteenth centuries to treatments in many languages in the thirteenth and fourteenth centuries. England, with only *Arthour and Merlin* and *Sir Tristrem* by the end of the thirteenth century seemingly shows a characteristic insular lateness, for its greatest Arthurian works are of the late fourteenth and the fifteenth centuries. When we remember, however, that the early courtly audience for romance in England would have been French[1] (an audience suitable for writers like Marie de France) we can see that the development of Arthurian romance in England is complex, representing both the growth of English as a literary language and a likely shift in the audience – or audiences – for romance.

Given the fact that they are part of the "Matter of Britain" and therefore, however distantly, reviving a native tradition, the English romances are extraordinarily derivative. Nearly all are retellings of French stories, sometimes whole works, as in Malory's translation of the *Queste del Saint Graal*, but often built from single episodes, as in the use made of small pieces from the first *Perceval* continuation in some of the Gawain romances. Given the importance of Chrétien's romances as material for translators, it is surprising that only *Ywain and Gawain* is a translation from Chrétien. Some of the writers were so unskilled that the current critical fashion for preferring texts to writers becomes attractive, although one is tempted to say that many of these works have more "inter-" than "textuality" about them. Nevertheless the English tradition also rose to undoubted masterpieces, chief among them *Sir Gawain and the Green Knight*, The Alliterative *Morte Arthure* and Malory's works. Many would add, as well, Chaucer's *Wife of Bath's Tale*, the Stanzaic *Morte Arthur* and *Ywain and Gawain*.

Because of the conventionality of the romances, even these masterpieces, it is not surprising that much of the scholarship in this field has attempted to circumscribe these conventions, to define the genre and set out what writers and audiences expected when they embarked on a romance quest.[2] In a symposium devoted to the vitality of the Arthurian legend, however, we must look in a different direction, for we want to seek a center, a point of life, in the English works in this tradition. I would like to come at this by looking first at the most recent study, Christopher Dean's *Arthur of England*, published just a few months ago.[3] Dean's work has a fairly straightforward thesis – that the Arthurian legends as a force in English medieval and Renaissance culture and literature aren't as important as they have been made to seem by several generations of enthusiastic scholars. He shows this by examining all English Arthurian works, by outlining all references to Arthur in "Non-Arthurian Literature," and also by listing all the early works in which there are simply no references to Arthur. He also demonstrates that Arthur's appearance does not always spell celebration, for the tradition includes a continuing critical treatment of Arthurian chivalry and a sometimes surprisingly negative treatment of Arthur and his court.

Dean shows us, I think, *not* that the Arthurian legends were not popular, but that *Arthur* was not always respected and that the uses to which Arthurian materials were put could vary quite widely. Thus we can say that the variety of subjects, forms and treatments in Middle English romance up through Malory's encyclopedic gathering together represents a drying up, in England, of the Arthurian stream. Indeed, Caxton's making available in print a complete account of the legends may have helped stop the flow, so that in spite of the popularity of Caxton's Malory, the legend of Arthur has almost no place in Renaissance English Literature. This process has been well described for later writers by Walter Jackson Bate in *The Burden of the Past and the English Poet*, and we can ask his eighteenth-century question of the Renaissance as well: After Malory, what was left to say about Arthur?[4]

Dean, of course, also shows the complicity of the humanists and their attitudes toward chivalric romance, summed up in Ascham's well-known view of the *Morte Darthur* as "open manslaughter and bold bawdry."[5] The upshot was that the Renaissance treatment of Arthur was slim and niggling: Arthur became a figure, in almost schematic terms, of Elizabethan pictorial mythography or of an allegorical system of values, but with very little vitality.

Spenser's *Faerie Queene* is the single Renaissance work of Arthurian inspiration which is energetic and accomplished. But the *Faerie Queene* is not usually taken seriously as Arthurian. It is not, after all, a *version* of any of the stories. Its authentication comes only through the appearance of Arthur, and thus it stands rather at the head of a line of modern works which are Arthurian because Merlin comes back to life or Excalibur is dug up somewhere.[6] Yet the *Faerie Queene* helps define the earlier tradition in a way that Malory or the modern works do not. Spenser's *Faerie Queene*, and not Malory, represents the culmination of the structural pattern of Arthurian romance, in which a knight rides out on a quest, but the quest reflects the growth and development of the knight himself. Spenser's knight-heroes learn, are tested and finally triumph, achieving perfection in individual virtues which, taken together, yield a pattern of courtesy. The visible standard of courtesy throughout the poem is Arthur, whose prowess measures out the virtues.

In the Middle English romances, Arthur is not the usual standard of courtesy. That role falls to Gawain, and it is in Gawain, I think, that we can find the vital center of English Arthurian romance.

Helaine Newstead, in her survey of Arthurian romance in Burke Severs's *Manual of Writing in Middle English*, identifies twelve romances as Gawain romances, and she is counting neither Chaucer's *Wife of Bath's Tale*, which surely retails a version of Gawain, nor works like the Alliterative *Morte Arthure*, which are about other characters but in which Gawain plays a central role.[7] The Gawain romances tend to be relatively short and they come into increasing prominence late in the period, so we can say that Gawain himself, while always centrally present in the Arthurian materials, gains stature as an individual English hero as the English romances establish an identity separate from the French cycle.

The Gawain romances display what seem to be characteristic English attitudes toward the legends. W.R.J. Barron summarizes these in "largely negative" terms based on the various superficial ways of classifying the romances; he finds:

> that English audiences preferred Gawain to Lancelot, that the Grail made little appeal to them... That English redactors fought shy of Chrétien, preferring the prose *Vulgate* and the *Perceval* continuations... That the English could not comprehend Courtly Love and preferred action to emotional analysis.[8]

These conclusions are augmented by a general sense of English moralism. Velma Richmond notes "the English regard for moral value";[9] Dieter Mehl, making the usual allowance for "freshness, charming simplicity and native rigour," also identifies a "strongly homiletic strain" which causes the English romances "almost from the beginning [to be] used as illustrations of certain moral and religious precepts."[10]

The Gawain romances participate in this Englishness in a rather specific way. As Lee Ramsey says in his recent book on *Chivalric Romances*:

> The usual story line shows Arthur's court, which represents the courtly establishment, subjected to a test or series of tests in which the chivalric Gawain takes up the main challenge. The significance of the tests varies considerably, but it is usually obvious. These are stories that express specific, though various, social doctrines or ideas.[11]

The plot, then, is an expression of idea. The English were comfortable with the romance structure, but as a model in which the quest is a search for meaning, or in which, as Peter Haidu says, "the hero rides out in search of semantic solutions."[12] Beneath the umbrella of the quest-meaning, the familiar romance form – "a sequence of minor adventures leading up to a major... adventure, usually announced from the beginning,"[13] – developed an episodic structure. The individual episodes are able to tease out meaning through two temporal structures: interrupted time and parallel time.

Interruption is one meaning underlying episodic structure. Within the romance the culminating adventure, the goal of the quest, provides a kind of temporal urgency for the hero, whose prowess is usually not in doubt. Interruptions shift the issue from his prowess to his judgment, which very well may be in doubt. The interruption in *Sir Gawain and the Green Knight* is the stay in Bercilak's castle, which, as an idyllic delay, in reality offers more opportunity for failure than does the apparent test facing Gawain, the inevitably fatal stroke of the Green Knight. In the Alliterative *Morte Arthure*, the interruption of Arthur's triumphant conquest of Europe is the demise of his fortunes at home, prepared for much earlier in the work. In *Ywain and Gawain*, the hero, whose marriage is interrupted by the call of chivalry, simply forgets to return home, choosing to live in the interruption.

Parallel movement is the more common way of investing episodic structure with meaning. Gawain's role in the romances was always intimately tied to a structure of contrast and juxtaposition. Through all the romances in the early Arthurian tradition, Gawain filled a structural role as foil or standard against which other knights could be measured. This was, indeed, part of his character, implicit in his heroism in the chronicle tradition (Geoffrey of Monmouth), and carried over into the structure of contrast in the earliest romances. It is interesting to note that both Gawain and Kay early developed identities which allowed them to stand as foils. Bedivere, who was also there from the Welsh beginnings, never really caught on and indeed, he has only become important as a replacement for Lancelot or as a narrator in modern novels by, say, Rosemary Sutcliff, Catherine Christian or Mary Stewart.14 In fact, in the chronicle tradition, as represented in the Alliterative *Morte Arthure*, Kay and Bedivere are killed early, in the campaign against Lucius, while Gawain is reserved for a hero's death near the end, fighting the archenemy.

Kay and Gawain were assigned their roles by the French and German writers. In the hands of Chrétien, Kay and Gawain come to serve thematic ends. Gawain's virtues are, in W.T.H. Jackson's words, "entirely secular – courage, loyalty, good breeding and chivalry both to men and women."15 Kay, on the other hand, represents an opposing field of values, for most often he is pretentious, bullying, small-minded and incompetent. These sets of values are entirely schematic: Gawain and Kay represent Arthurian chivalry at its best and at its worst.

In the form of the works, Gawain and Kay are like polar magnets which exert the force of their values on the hero-knights whose characters are being defined and refined in the works. Kay propels the adventure out of the court as surely as if Chrétien wanted to show that adventures start through a failure in chivalry. In *Knight of the Cart* Kay cynically manipulates Arthur into entrusting the Queen into his hands and thus into hazard. In *Perceval*, Kay sends the unlikely young rustic in dangerous pursuit of the Red Knight. Gawain, in both works, stands over against the title heroes during the quests, performing parallel actions so that the status of the hero can be measured. Kay and Gawain, it must be understood, represent aspects of Arthur himself, the contradictory impulses present in chivalry from the beginning. Kay, as the false Arthur, usurps Arthur's role as husband and protector in *Knight of the Cart*, and in *Perceval* stands in Arthur's place as sanctioner of quests. Gawain, a kind of true Arthur – truer, in fact, than Arthur himself – assumes in Chrétien the role Spenser assigned to Arthur in the *Faerie Queene,* a role actually implicit in the figure of Arthur from his very first appearance in the *Gododdin* (c. 600), when Aneirin praises the hero Gwarddur, but finds that "he was not Arthur."16 Gawain represents for the individual knight both the belief in perfectibility and the standard of perfection.

The displacement of Arthur by Kay and Gawain itself serves a thematic function in the works. The essential absence of Arthur in *Knight of the Cart* allows Lancelot, the lover of the Queen, to seem wedded to her morally. In these terms love, and not simply the prowess figured in Gawain, becomes the true issue for judgment in the romance. In the crucial episode of the three-day tournament, Lancelot's willingness to humiliate himself, to place prowess entirely at the service of love, redefines knightly success in terms that are beyond the capacity of Gawain to understand, and therefore beyond his figural meaning. In *Perceval* the absence of Arthur redoubles the meaning of the elaborate contrast of Perceval with Gawain. Against Perceval's naiveté, Gawain exemplifies perfection of martial techniques, the reputation of accomplishment, and experience in love. But he cannot represent fatherhood, as Arthur could, and Arthur's virtual absence enforces a recognition of the spiritual lineage that is missing to the fatherless Perceval.

Nowhere is the polarity between Kay and Gawain clearer than in the blood-in-the-snow episode. In all versions of this story a surly Kay is unseated by the pensive Perceval, while a courteous Gawain considerately talks him back into court.

Even the English *Sir Perceval of Galles*, which lacks the blood-in-the-snow episode, makes up the lack by establishing the contrast at the start of the romance. The god-like knights whom the young Perceval meets in the forest include "Gawaine with honour" and "Kay, þe bolde baratour" [bully] (261-62).17 The text then reinforces the contrast by countering Kay's insolent speech to the boy with Gawain's courtesy: Sir Gawain answers "faire and curtaisely," he is called "meke and mylde/ And softe of ansuare" (291-92), and he rebukes Kay for his "prowde wordes" (306).

In *The Green Knight*, a late and imperfect condensation of *Sir Gawain and the Green Knight* in the Bishop Percy Folio MS, Kay is given an expanded role, to heighten the effect of Gawain's assumption of the Green Knight's challenge. When Kay immediately accepts the contest the Green Knight proposes, he is rebuked by the other knights as a swaggerer, as if this were the way he always foolishly talked. At the beginning of the work, the Green Knight has, in fact, already announced to us his intention to test Gawain, not Arthur or the court, so we are aware of Kay's disruption of narrative focus even as he opens his mouth and even though his words are not particularly brash, by saga standards.

The Carl of Carlisle could be seen as a virtual transformation into boisterous English action of what is static and emblematic in the French blood-in-the-snow episode. Kay, Gawain, and the Bishop Baldwin ask to spend the night with the churlish Carl. Bishop Baldwin, checking on his horse, impetuously pushes the Carl's foal out of the stable where his horse is feeding. Sir Kay is once again surly and mouthy, and he beats the foal and drives it away from his own horse. Kay's behavior is intended to illuminate Gawain's perfect courtesy, which extends to people and animals alike. Gawain courteously takes the foal back into the stable where his horse is feeding. Furthermore, Gawain responds to all the host's demands with perfect obedience, which fulfills the terms of an earlier vow of the host. For his reward, after he is tempted in bed by the host's wife in a strangely misguided test, Gawain is given the Carl's daughter, both as bed-partner and as wife.

Even while they demonstrate the continuity of the contrast between Kay and

Gawain, these English works are no longer like the French ones. In their similarities we see how deeply embedded in Arthurian romance is the role of Gawain, so that a repetition of the form calls forth a repetition of the character. But "character" as such is not really at issue: it is *meaning* that is being made manifest in the repetition of Gawain. It is this strong sense of the formal and functional in Gawain that causes readers to find the abstract, the exemplary, even the allegorical in Gawain.[18] Yet a close look at the differences in these English and French manifestations of Gawain shows that his reappearance is not a serial activity, the simple borrowing or translating of something from an earlier work in a chronological development. The repetition of Gawain is rather more a vertical than a horizontal process. Literary theorists have recently begun to specify the significance of repetition in a medieval context. Peter Haidu, for instance, has seen medieval repetition taking the form

> of a further concretization, a further incorporation and revelation of the abstract and the Idea. Repetition is referred not to the chain of history but to the chain of being. It is referred to the abstract Form that gives meaning and validity to each of the particular concretizations; each repetition therefore constitutes a further revelation of value, since it brings before our eyes again that aspect of the abstract Form that can be concretized and visualized.[19]

This is a highly Platonic subscribing of genre: an idea or story – or in this case, a *figure* – is repeated because in its form it is true, and its repetition both reveals and reinsures its value. The range of ideas of Gawain can then be disclosed through a reexamination of some key texts.

In the structure of the French romances, first of all, a thematic pattern of growth and development fosters the increasing coherence in the career of the hero-knight. The structural pattern of contrast also supports this theme, for we see the incomplete hero always in the light of the *finished* knight, Gawain. But of course, contrast cuts both ways, and the growth of Lancelot and of Perceval exposes the limitations of the secular courtliness of Gawain. Lancelot's chivalry refined by love-service is superior (in the morally circumscribed world of the text) to Gawain's simple martial values, which leave him floundering in the water while Lancelot crosses the sword bridge. That Gawain's contrast with Lancelot is limited and does not effect a complete denigration of the chivalric values figured in Gawain is clearly shown by the additional contrast between Lancelot and Meleagant. Meleagant is an unscrupulous knight whose deep insecurity leads to his failure in the basic commitments of chivalry. These commitments, we are to understand, are shared equally by Lancelot and by Gawain. Gawain, whatever his failure, would never fall short of the ideals in *that* way.

Perceval's special destiny with respect to the Grail transforms his chivalry in spiritual terms increasingly superior to the grounds of Gawain's actions. Excluded from the realm of spiritual meaning, Gawain undertakes a series of parallel adventures which, in the light of the redefined ethos, seem increasingly aimless and time-bound.

In these French romances, then, chivalry is refined and redefined in the meaning of the title hero. His values come to surpass the standard chivalry of the static Gawain through an identification with what we might call a *religious* dynamic, if we are willing to accept the refined religion of love which informs Lancelot's worship of his lady as a syntactic equivalent to Perceval's slow recognition of the meaning of his quest. That the two are not *semantically* equivalent is exposed in the fact that the two Gawains are not really the same – they are, rather, repetitions of Gawain, each asserting only an aspect of the failure of Arthurian chivalry. The devaluation of Gawain in *Knight of the Cart* is comic, revealing the rejection of self-centeredness in the textual world of love. In *Perceval*, Gawain's failure is existential and potentially tragic, as the self-centeredness of his values is weighed against the spiritual call of the Other in the Grail.

The English repetitions of Gawain transform these meanings, as I have suggested. In the first place, the narrative focus shifts away from a young hero, intent on his quest and enacting an education into redefined chivalry. In the English romances, the episodes implying a contrast entangle Arthur's companions, and Gawain is made the standard by which we judge other "finished" knights of the Round Table. As we saw earlier, the contrast with Kay is most common, but Gawain also shows Arthur to bad advantage in *Golagros and Gawain* and in the *Awowing of King Arthur*. Bishop Baldwin, as we saw, is exposed in *Gawain and the Carl of Carlisle*. That they are "finished" means that these knights do not grow or even change, but are themselves cardboard representations. In this way the English romances become an examination of behavior pure and simple: courtesy itself, and its public projection, reputation, are at issue in these romances. When there is only a single hero, as in *Sir Gawain and the Green Knight, The Green Knight, The Wedding of Sir Gawain and Dame Ragnell*, and *The Adventures at the Tarn Wadling*, to name a few, this emphasis on courtly behavior causes the hero, Gawain, to be measured against his own standards, or against his reputation.

This emphasis on behavior is made all the more striking in that for both structures – the single hero romance and the romance of contrast – there is an example of an inversion, which manifests Gawain in thoroughly negative terms. In Malory's story of Pelleas and Ettarde, for instance, Gawain offers to help Pelleas win the woman of his dreams. Pelleas's former strategy, gaining her attention by public humiliation in a series of daily battles he deliberately loses, has not worked. Gawain the go-between, entering the castle supposedly on

Pelleas's behalf, ends up in Ettarde's bed, seriously betraying his trust. The story ends in a nice combination of *Sir Launfal* and *Midsummer Night's Dream*, for the Lady of the Lake, admiring Pelleas's qualities, takes him off to a lover's fantasy otherworld, but not before causing Ettarde to love him in turn, now without hope. Gawain, adopting the familiar structural position of exemplar, turns out to be the one weighed, and we see his scale fall in contrast with the true and gentle Pelleas.

The inversion played on Gawain as hero of his own romance occurs in the strange little work, *The Jest of Gawain*. For virtually the entire text, Gawain is making love to an unnamed girl, leaving her bed only to fight with her father and each of her three brothers in turn. While we may at first find our sympathies engaged on the side of the family who are offended at the couple's behavior, we soon abandon sympathy altogether. Gawain, who defeats the father and the first two brothers, fights to an ignominious draw with Sir Brandles, the third brother. As Gawain trundles abashed out of the romance in one direction, Brandles beats his sister up and drives her off in the other direction as a strumpet, a conclusion which finds little favor with the very small modern audience for this tale. As with *Pelleas and Ettarde*, this slight romance follows closely the debased view of Gawain in its French sources.

The conventionality of the structural forms of these repetitions, and the loss of the "growth of the hero" as a thematic focus, should not cause us to miss the subtlety of meaning which English texts derive from the figure of Gawain. To demonstrate this point, let me conclude this paper by looking in more detail at three complex repetitions of Gawain. The first two occur in examples of the structural pattern I have been calling the romance of contrast, *The Avowing of Arthur* and the Alliterative *Morte Arthure*. The third repetition is the narrative center of *Sir Gawain* and *the Green Knight*, a masterfully structured single-hero romance. The meaning of Gawain in each of these works illuminates English romance more generally.

In *The Avowing of King Arthur*, the first part of the text is a very conventional set of romance adventures, motivated by the boasting vows made by Arthur, Kay and Gawain. Arthur vows to kill a boar, Kay to ride around Inglewood Forest, and Gawain to keep watch all night at the Tarn Wadling. The fulfillment of the boar hunt is the kind of celtic heroic action which clings to Arthur from primeval times. Kay's action characteristically lands him on the ground, the captive of the potent knight, Sir Menealfe of the Mountain. Gawain spends *his* part of the adventure rescuing both Kay and a young lady from the clutches of Sir Menealfe, whose martial qualities Gawain recognizes, and whose services he gains on Arthur's behalf. The second part of the romance is devoted to the fulfilling of the rather complicated set of three vows made at the start of the poem by the fourth member of Arthur's party, Sir Baldwin of Britain. As the poem's most recent editor, Roger Dahood, has pointed out, the second part is very different from the first in that Baldwin does not seek adventure and in that the six episodes showing him first being tested against his vows and then recounting the explanations for the three vows are heavily didactic, with an emphasis on proverbial wisdom and philosophical meaning.[20] For our purpose, two points are important. First, Arthur and Kay themselves set out to test Baldwin, who has vowed never to suspect his wife, by "planting" a naked knight in her bed while Baldwin is away and pretending to hold him there until Baldwin's return. This bed test, in its comic preoccupations and its portrayal of the king himself as a kind of roisterous practical joker, is out of keeping with the philosophical significance which the text attaches to Baldwin's vows.

Because the bed test has parallels involving Gawain himself in *Gawain and the Carl of Carlisle* and *Sir Gawain and the Green Knight*, we are reminded, second, that Gawain is absent from this part of the poem. This absence is particularly signigicant since Gawain's usual place would be in the bed with the wife, an association the text suppresses by making Arthur's pawn in this game an unnamed lackey. It is hard to avoid the conclusion that this text, having in the first part shown the prowess of the romance Gawain, believes him to be above the shenanigans of the second part. These same games, however, are quite in celtic keeping with the exploits of a boar-hunting king.

The significance of Gawain's absence here can remind us similarly that other of the repetitions of Gawain are *not* Gawain. Chaucer's *Wife of Bath's Tale*, focusing on a hero who is a repetition of Gawain, suppresses the identification, perhaps because of the rape which sets events in motion, but also because the long speech on "gentilesse" delivered by the hag on their wedding night would seem inappropriate addressed to the English exemplar of courtesy. The analogue in *The Wedding of Gawain and Dame Ragnell*, it should be remembered, shows Gawain as a figure of magnanimity, who takes on both the question-quest and the marriage to the hag on Arthur's behalf.

Libeaus Desconus, I would argue, is also a Gawain romance. The story of the "fair unknown," with versions in French and Italian, its hero is Gingalyn, Gawain's son. Here Gawain does not take on his usual structural role through a series of parallel adventures. Instead he arms the boy at the beginning and sends him out on adventure. We can interpret the quest as a projection forward onto his son of Gawain's own *enfances*, necessary because Gawain's textual form is completeness, not growth. Among his adventures is an enchanted stay for a year with the Dame de l'amour, a magical reification of the forward ladies common in Gawain's own adventures and from whose spell Gingalyn must free himself before he can, like Odysseus escaping from Circe, achieve the wife at the end of his quest.

The Alliterative *Morte Arthure*, now generally acknowledged to be a masterpiece of Middle English literature, poses an unusually rich set of meanings for a work which depends heavily upon the chronicle tradition. In Dean's view, the Alliterative *Morte Arthure* is "a chronicle-type romance" that "uses much of the chronicle subject matter and that shares something of that tradition's view of Arthur."[21] Arthur *is* the clear hero of the poem, but Gawain's role is so significant, especially in the last half of the poem, that Thorlac Turville-Petre sees Arthur *and* Gawain as protagonists.[22] Jörg Fichte has studied the figure of Gawain in some detail,[23] and he sees the meaning of Gawain in essentially negative terms: a comparison with Geoffrey, Layamon, and Wace, Fichte argues, shows that the poet has taken great pains to narrow Gawain's range of values and to strip him of any possible reliance on wisdom and counsel. Fichte notes the continual associations of Gawain with violence and impetuosity. In the medieval model which sees the ideal hero as balanced between *sapientia* and *fortitudo*, Fichte believes that Gawain figures forth an unmixed *fortitudo* and thus stands as a figure of contrast by which we can judge the wisdom of Arthur himself, especially near the end of the poem when Arthur has the potential of rising to a kind of redeemed tragic stature.

Fichte is correct, I believe, in noting the changes from the sources which seem to narrow Gawain's range of values; he also rightly assesses Gawain's association with impetuosity. Nevertheless, I think Gawain's role in the poem is more complex and his meaning more ambiguous than Fichte allows.

The playoff between *sapientia* and *fortitudo* in earlier heroic literature is usually structured in one of two clear ways. In the first, the qualities are split between contrasting characters like Roland and Oliver. As the *Song of Roland* itself says, "Roland is fierce and Oliver is wise / And both for valour may bear away the prize."[24] As we saw earlier in the comparison between Gawain and Lancelot, simple valor is not the point of comparison; rather we are concerned with the source of judgment and control, the mediation of reason and passion. The poem *Beowulf* figures the two qualities – *sapientia* and *fortitudo* – in the single hero, and not only shows us the mix at the prime age of the young hero in his most glorious exploit, but also contrasts his impetuous youth (the swimming contest with Breca) and his old age, when as king he must face the dragon of his death. The Alliterative *Morte Arthure* shows the balance of the two forces in the figure of Arthur. But as critics have long noticed, the degree of sapiential control exhibited by Arthur varies quite widely, from the figure of wisdom in the council, to the Beowulfian hero on St. Michael's Mount, to the aggressive and vindictive warrior during the siege of Metz.

The rash extreme playing off against the changing Arthur is not Gawain, but Sir Cador, I believe. Cador, as Arthur's heir, speaks first in the council, expressing his unabashed joy that war has finally come again. Arthur upbraids him, but with good humor:

"Sir Cador," quod the king, "thy counsel is noble;
But thou art a marvelous man with thy merry wordes!
For thou countes no case ne castes no further
But hurles forth upon heved, as thy herte thinkes. (259-62)[25]

[Sir Cador," said the King, "your counsel is worthy;
What a wondrous one you are with your glad words,
For you reckon no risk nor reflect any further,
But rush forth to the fore, as your heart bids.]

The true sign of Cador's rashness comes, however, when he is entrusted with the hostage party and foolishly engages the enemy who are waiting in ambush. Cador's motive for risking his men is unselfconsciously announced:

It were shame that we sholde shoun for so little!
Sir Launcelot shall never laugh, that with the king lenges,
That I sholde let my way for lede upon erthe. (1719-21)

[It would be shame for us to shrink for so little;
Sir Lancelot, back with the King, shall never laugh,
That I quit my path for any person on earth!]

Cador speaks of shame in the old heroic way, and his fear of the laughter of the fellowship of knights forces his choice. Arthur attacks his decision:

Sir Cador, thy corage confoundes us all!
Cowardly thou castes out all my best knightes!
To put men in peril, it is no pris holden,
But the parties were purveyed and power arrayed;
When thou were stedde on a strenghe thou sholde have withstonden,
But yif ye wolde all my steren stroy for the nones! (1922-27)

[Sir Cador, your courage will ruin us all!
Basely you are bringing down all my best knights;
To put men in peril is prized as no virtue,
Unless both sides be ready with forces arrayed.
Safe in a stronghold you should have taken your stand,
Unless you wish to destroy all my stalwarts for good!]

Gawain's performance must be seen not only in the light of Arthur's transformation in the poem, but also in contrast to Cador. Gawain is shown acting four times in the poem. At the beginning of the poem, after the banquet for the ambassadors, the party is returning to chambers, and "Sir Gawain the worthy Dame Waynor he ledes" (233). In his second appearance, Gawain is himself leading the embassage to Lucius. After an exchange of taunts, Gawain rashly lops off the head of Sir Gayous in the presence of the Emperor. In his third major action, Gawain is sent on a foraging party to plunder food for the hungry troops. Discovering a knight at a stream, Gawain quickly engages him in the kind of meaningless single combat common in the romances, a dangerous flexing of muscles to determine masculine dominance. Through this combat Gawain enlists Sir Priamus in Arthur's cause against the Duke of Lorraine. Gawain's fourth appearance is his landing on the shore of Britain and his premature engagement with Mordred, who slaughters him slyly.

These four episodes are not of a kind; they are, rather, four different repetitions of Gawain representing four different aspects of Arthurian heroism. A complete argument is not possible here, but I would suggest that Gawain figures forth the hero in four generically different traditions related to the story of Arthur. When he accompanies Guinevere to the banquet, he is the knight of courtesy, the special protector of the Queen, and the pair of them contrast with the coupling of treachery Mordred and Guinevere make near the end. The rash attack upon Gayous in Lucius's court is the action of the impetuous hero of the saga or *chanson de geste*. If Gawain shares qualities here with Roland, he also partakes of the impetuosity of Malory's Balin, who smites down the Lady of the Lake in Arthur's presence, without forethought and without regard for consequences. The episode with Sir Priamus is a pure romance interlude, placed in a landscape which is incongruously idyllic and removed from the conflict of larger social forces in the poem. Jousting with an unknown opponent is a typically aimless and irrational romantic action, and in the context of this poem it is difficult to account for. It is only incidental to the impending battle with the Duke of Lorraine, although Gawain's enlisting of Priamus on Arthur's side is its putative justification. It also functions to create a romance-in-small, in which the larger defeat of the forces of Lorraine is foreshadowed in the exquisite game of two exemplars of chivalry, the epic battle pre-staged in the refined realm of romance. But the episode is also like a medallion, set directly parallel to Arthur's single combat earlier in the poem, when he defeats the giant of St. Michael's Mount. The Priamus episode enforces a comparison of the two heroes, the aimlessness of Gawain's romance adventure pointing up the Christian purpose with which Arthur engaged the giant. That the comparison is intended by the poet is shown in the earlier episode. Kay and Bedivere – not Gawain– accompany Arthur on his solitary mission, but when the old lady tries to warn Arthur away, she says:

> Weenes thou to britten him with thy brand rich?
> Were thou wighter than Wade or Wawain either,
> Thou winnes no worship, I warn thee before. (963-65)

[Do you hope to slay him with your stout sword?
Be you stronger than Wade or even than Gawain,
You will reap no renown, I warn you beforehand.]

The fourth appearance, Gawain's death at Mordred's hands, mirrors Arthur's death and thus thematically links the two in the fated world of the tragic hero. Certainly the long eulogies over the dead Gawain delivered by *both* Mordred and Arthur have the effect of raising him to that stature: there will, after all, be no one to speak at Arthur's death. Even the poet's interjection that Gawain would have been luckier had he kept to his strong position on the hilltop (3768-69) can be read, not as an attack upon Gawain's strategy in the battle, but as a bewailing of the misfortune which inevitably follows.

These appearances of Gawain, in which he enacts the varieties of chivalric action, reinforce the generic shiftiness of this remarkable poem. Gawain can be seen to represent, within the text, the possibilities of significant action in the Arthurian world, and the quest of meaning for generic form.[26]

While Gawain's reputation is a force in all these works, no romance makes the issue of reputation so explicitly a part of the action as *Sir Gawain and the Green Knight*. Each stage of the narrative is propelled by a challenge based on the failure of Arthur's knights to live up to their renown. The Green Knight, seeing no response to his first offer of a game, asks whether he is really in Arthurs court, a humiliating jibe that brings the shamed king to his feet. During the three days of temptation, the lady shames Gawain into kissing her by suggesting:

> Bot þat ʒe be Gawan hit gotʒ in mynde ...
> Sir, ʒif ʒe be Wawen, wonder me þynkkeʒ
> Wyʒe þat is so wel wrast alway to god
> And conneʒ not of compaynye þe costeʒ vndertake. (1293, 1481-83)[27]

> [But that you are Gawain ceases to exist in (my) mind ...
> Sir, if you are Gawain, (it) seems amazing to me
> (That a) knight who is so much inclined always toward good deeds
> Also can not comprehend the customs of courtesy.]

The same challenge is used by the Green Knight at the end when Gawain is seen to flinch from the first blow:

> "þou art not Gawayn," quoþ þe gome, "þat is so goud halden,
> þat neuer arʒed for no here by hylle ne be vale,
> And now þou fles for ferde er þou fele harmeʒ." (2270-72)

["You can not be Gawain," said the man, "who is considered so great,
Who never shuddered before any group on hill or in vale,
If now you flinch with fear before you feel injuries."]

The challenge for Gawain is not simply behaving courteously. It is rather living up to the expectations of those whose standards have been set by his reputation. When Gawain first arrives at Bercilak's castle, he is welcomed by the provincial knights as the very standard of courtesy. At last they can see how table manners and conversations are conducted at the king's court:

Now schal we semlych se sleȝ teȝ of þeweȝ,
And þe teccheles termes of talkyng noble;
Wich spede is in speche vnspurd may we lerne,
Syn we haf fonged þat fyne fader of nurture. (916-19)

[Now we shall properly perceive modes of chivalrous acts,
And the flawless phrases of noble conversation;
We may learn without inquiring what power (there) is in speech,
Since we have received that fine father of good breeding.]

If the poet shows us the insecurity of these country courtiers who are trying to pull on the fashionable garments of an alien behavior, he also shows us that Gawain's courtesy and reputation have become his integrity. When the guide leading him to the Green Chapel offers him the chance to escape with his life *and* his reputation, Gawain refuses, saying:

Bot helde þou hit neuer so holde, and I here passed,
Founded for ferde for to fle in fourme þat þou telleȝ,
I were a knyȝt kowarde; I myȝt not be excused. (2129-31)

[But (even if) you kept it ever so loyally, and I now departed,
Traveling in fear to flee in (the) way that you say,
I would be a cowardly knight; I could not be excused.]

The public shame that propelled Arthur early in the poem or Sir Cador in the Alliterative *Morte Arthure* is here a matter of private conscience. Gawain's view of himself, his reading of his own meaning, arises from a necessary integrity of performance, in which reputation has been internalized and raised into a standard of behavior. This may explain why Gawain unleashes his vitriolic and uncourteous attack upon feminine wiles when he discovers he has been tricked. Gawain was aware of two tests, really: first, the private test of courtesy with the forward lady, and, second, the dispiriting public test of prowess with the Green Knight, which will lead to his certain death. His moment of greatest triumph comes – so he believes – when, the first test behind him, he thinks he has also passed the second test: he joyfully draws his sword for what will finally be an even fight. Gawain has not, after all, been like Perceval; he has *not* been simply muddling through. He has done well because he knows what he is doing, because they all were right when they said those wonderful things about him. And then the ground shifts. It is the student's double nightmare: he had taken a test he didn't know about, and the exam he prepared for didn't count!

At this moment of exposure, Gawain takes his place among other romance heroes. Looking at traditional romance heroes, Frederic Jameson has suggested:

> that the hero's dominant trait is naiveté or inexperience, and that his most characteristic posture is that of bewilderment. Surely, far from being an emissary of the 'upper world,' the hero of romance is something closer to an observer, a mortal spectator surprised by supernatural conflict, who then himself is gradually drawn in, to reap the rewards of victory without even quite being aware of what was at stake in the first place.[28]

Jameson's identification applies pointedly to Gawain, who is suddenly "a mortal spectator surprised by supernatural conflict." This Knight of the Virgin and the Pentangle, the Knight of Certainty, is forcibly transformed at the end of the poem into the first Knight of the Green Sash, the Knight of Bewilderment.

Because we are all – we moderns – fully invested members of the Order of Bewilderment, this Gawain is, for most of us, the most vital of Middle English Gawains. But I hope I have shown the extent to which he is a repetition, a reenactment of complex meanings. Some of these meanings seem inextricable from the form and structure of romance. Others draw their life from a tradition of expectations which grew up around Arthur and his companions. And finally, some of these meanings are notably English, and make Gawain the central figure in the English imagination of Arthur. In Gawain's repetitions we can trace the vitality of the English Arthurian legends.

Works cited

Ascham, Roger. "The Schoolmaster." *The Golden Hind*. Revised Edition. Ed. Roy Lamson and Hallett Smith. New York: Norton, 1956. 79-112.

Barron, W.R.J. "Arthurian Romance: Traces of an English Tradition."*English Studies* 6 (1980): 2-23.

Bate, Walter Jackson. *The Burden of the Past and the English Poet*. Harvard University Press, 1970 [rpt. New York: Norton, 1972],

Benson, Larry D., ed. *King Arthur's Death: The Middle English Stanzaic*

Morte Arthur and Alliterative Morte Arthure. Indianapolis: Bobbs-Merrill, 1974.

Boardman, Phillip C. "Arthur *Redivivus*: A Reader's Guide to Recent Arthurian Fiction." *Halcyon* 2 (1980): 41-56.

Brunner, Karl. "Middle English Metrical Romances and Their Audience." *Studies in Medieval Literature in Honor of Professor Albert Croll Baugh.* Ed. MacEdward Leach. Philadelphia: Univeristy of Pennsylvania Press, 1961. 219-27.

Christian, Catherine. *The Pendragon* [British title: *The Sword and the Flame*]. New York: Alfred A. Knopf, 1979.

Crane, Susan. *Insular Romance: Politics, Faith, and Culture in Anglo-Norman and Middle English Literature.* Berkeley: University of California Press, 1986.

Dahood, Roger, ed. *The Awowing of King Arthur.* New York: Garland, 1984.

Dean, Christopher. *Arthur of England: English Attitudes to King Arthur and the Knights of the Round Table in the Middle Ages and the Renaissance.* Toronto: University of Toronto Press, 1987.

Everett, Dorothy. *Essays on Middle English Literature.* Ed. Patricia Kean. Oxford: Clarendon Press, 1955.

Finlayson, J. "The Expectations of Romance in *Sir Gawain and the Green Knight.*" *Genre* 12 (1979): 1-24.

French, Walter Hoyt and Charles Brockway Hale, eds. *Middle English Metrical Romances.* 2 Vols. New York: Russell and Russell, 1964 [1930].

Frye, Northrop. *Anatomy of Criticism: Four Essays.* Princeton: Princeton University Press, 1957.

Göller, Karl Heinz, ed. *The Alliterative Morte Arthure: A Reassessment of the Poem.* Cambridge: D.S. Brewer, 1981.

Haidu, Peter, ed. *Approaches to Medieval Romance. Yale French Studies* 51 (1974).

Haidu, Peter. "Repetition: Modern Reflections on Medieval Aesthetics." *MLN* 92 (1977): 875-87.

Hume, Kathryn. "The Formal Nature of Middle English Romance." *Philological Quarterly* 53 (1974): 158-80.

Jackson, W.T.H. "The Arthuricity of Marie de France." *Romanic Review* 70 (1979): 1-18.

Jameson, Fredric. "Magical Narratives: Romance as Genre." *New Literary History* 7 (1975): 135-163.

Jost, Jean E. *Ten Middle English Arthurian Romances: A Reference Guide.* Boston: G.K. Hall, 1986.

Krishna, Valerie, trans. *The Alliterative Morte Arthure: A New Verse Translation.* Washington, D.C.: University Press of America, 1983.

Laubenthal, Sanders Anne. *Excalibur.* New York: Ballantine, 1973.

Lewis, C.S. *That Hideous Strength: A Modern Fairy-Tale for Grown-ups.* London: The Bodley Head, 1945.

Mathewson, Jeanne T. "Displacement of the Feminine in *Golagros and Gawane* and the *Awntyrs off Arthure.*" *Arthurian Interpretations* 1.2 (1987): 23-28.

Mehl, Dieter. *The Middle English Romances of the Thirteenth and Fourteenth Centuries.* London: Routledge and Kegan Paul, 1968 [German Edition 1967].

Nichols, Stephen G., Jr. "Solomon's Wife: Deceit, Desire, and the Genealogy of Romance." *Space, Time, Image, Sign: Essays on Literature and the Visual Arts.* Ed. James A.W. Heffernan. New York: Peter Lang, 1987. 19-40.

Norman, Diana. *King of the Last Days.* London: Hodder and Stoughton, 1981.

Pearsall, Derek. "The Development of Middle English Romance." *Mediæval Studies* 27 (1965): 91-116.

Pearsall, Derek. "The English Romance in the Fifteenth Century." *Essays and Studies* 29 (1976): 56-83.

Ramsey, Lee C. *Chivalric Romances: Popular Literature in Medieval England.* Bloomington: Indiana University Press, 1983.

Richmond, Velma Bourgeois. *The Popularity of Middle English Romance.* Bowling Green, Ohio: Bowling Green University Popular Press, 1975.

Sayers, Dorothy, trans. *The Song of Roland.* Harmondsworth: Penguin, 1957.

Severs, J. Burke, editor. *A Manual of Writings in Middle English 1050-1500.* New Haven:Connecticut Academy of Arts and Sciences, 1967.

Stewart, Mary. *The Wicked Day.* New York: William Morrow, 1983.

Sutcliff, Rosemary. *Sword at Sunset.* New York: Coward-McCann, 1963.

Turville-Petre, Thorlac. *The Alliterative Revival.* Cambridge: D.S. Brewer, 1977.

Wilhelm, James J. and Laila Zamuelis Gross, eds. *The Romance of Arthur.* New York: Garland, 1984.

Wittig, Susan. *Stylistic and Narrative Structures in the Middle English Romances.* Austin: University of Texas Press, 1978.

Notes

[1] In *Insular Romance: Politics, Faith, and Culture in Anglo-Norman and Middle English Literature* (Berkeley: University of California Press, 1986), Susan Crane notes the close connection between Anglo-Norman romance and the Middle English romances about English heroes. She generally ignores Arthurian legend, but does treat Thomas's *Tristan* and *Sir Tristrem*.

[2] For examples of sometimes striking approaches to these traditional questions, see cited

works in the Bibliography by Barron, Brunner, Everett, Finlayson, Frye, Hume, Jameson, Nichols, Pearsall, and Wittig. Jean E. Jost, in *Ten Middle English Arthurian Romances: A Reference Guide* (Boston: G.K. Hall, 1986), provides an annotated survey of criticism for the most important Middle English romances, excluding Chaucer, Malory and *Sir Gawain and the Green Knight*. These last have been widely surveyed in a number of sources, including annual bibliographies, individual reference guides, and handbooks.

[3] *Arthur of England: English Attitudes to King Arthur and the Knights of the Round Table in the Middle Ages and the Renaissance* (Toronto: University of Toronto Press, 1987).

[4] *The Burden of the Past and the English Poet* (New York: Norton, 1972).

[5] "The Schoolmaster," in *The Golden Hind* (Rev. edition), ed. Roy Lamson and Hallett Smith (New York: Norton, 1956): 107.

[6] In C.S. Lewis's *That Hideous Strength* (London: The Bodley Head, 1945), for instance, Merlin returns frighteningly to life when his cave is excavated in the gardens of a provincial college. Diana Norman's *King of the Last Days* (London: Hodder and Stoughton, 1981) shows Excalibur found at Glastonbury during the reign of Henry II, while in *Excalibur* (New York: Ballantine, 1973), by Sanders Anne Laubenthal, it appears much more recently in Mobile, Alabama. For a discussion of these tangential Arthurian works, see Phillip C. Boardman, "Arthur *Redivivus:* A Reader's Guide to Recent Arthurian Fiction," *Halcyon* 2 (1980): 41-56.

[7] "Arthurian Legends" in J. Burke Severs, editor, *A Manual of Writings in Middle English 1050-1500* (New Haven: Connecticut Academy of Arts and Sciences, 1967): 53-70.

[8] "Arthurian Romance: Traces of an English Tradition." *English Studies* 6 (1980): 5.

[9] Velma Bourgeois Richmond, *The Popularity of Middle English Romance* (Bowling Green, Ohio: Bowling Green University Popular Press, 1975): 121.

[10] *The Middle English Romances of the Thirteenth and Fourteenth Centuries* (London: Routledge and Kegan Paul, 1968 [German Edition 1967]): 1-2, 19.

[11] *Chivalric Romances: Popular Literature in Medieval England* (Bloomington: Indiana University Press, 1983): 200.

[12] "Introduction," *Approaches to Medieval Romance (Yale French Studies* 51): 5.

[13] Northrop Frye, *The Anatomy of Criticism: Four Essays* (Princeton: Princeton University Press): 186-87.

[14] Bedivere is the narrator in Christian's *The Pendragon* (New York: Alfred A. Knopf, 1979). In both Sutcliff's *Sword at Sunset* (New York: Coward-McCann, 1963) and Stewart's *The Wicked Day* (New York: William Morrow, 1983), Bedwyr replaces Lancelot as Arthur's closest friend and lover of the queen.

[15] "The Nature of Romance" in Haidu, ed., *YFS* 51: 20. Elsewhere, Jackson says of Chrétien's Gawain: "He is brave, generous, and always ready to recognize the good in other people. He is devoted to the code of love-supremacy and the pursuit of individual honor" ("The Arthuricity of Marie de France," *Romanic Review* 70 (1979): 3).

[16] The relevant passage, in a translation by John K. Bollard, is excerpted in *The Romance of Arthur*, ed. James J. Wilhelm and Laila Zamuelis Gross (New York: Garland, 1984): 14.

[17] "Sir Perceval of Galles" in *Middle English Metrical Romances,* ed. Walter Hoyt French and Charles Brockway Hale (New York: Russell and Russell, 1964 [1930]): II.540.

[18] Jeanne T. Mathewson, for instance, argues in "Displacement of the Feminine in *Golagros and Gawane* and the *Awntyrs off Arthure*" (*Arthurian Interpretations* 1.2 [1987]: 26) that Gawain and Arthur are "allegorical figures in a morality play" in *Golagros and Gawain*.

[19] "Repetition: Modern Reflections on Medieval Aesthetics," *MLN* 92 [1977]: 880.

[20] *The Avowing of King Arthur* (New York: Garland, 1984): 36-37.

21 Dean: 70.

22 *The Alliterative Revival* (Cambridge: D.S. Brewer, 1977): 102.

23 "The Figure of Sir Gawain" in *The Alliterative Morte Arthure: A Reassessment of the Poem,* ed. Karl Heinz Göller (Cambridge: D.S. Brewer, 1981): 106-16.

24 *Chanson de Roland,* Laisse 87; here trans. Dorothy Sayers, *The Song of Roland* (Harmondsworth: Penguin, 1957): 94.

25 All passages from the Alliterative *Morte Arthure* are from the Middle English text in Larry D. Benson's *King Arthur's Death* (Indianapolis: Bobbs-Merrill, 1974) and are cited parenthetically in the text by line number. Translations of those cited lines are given from Valerie Krishna's *The Alliterative Morte Arthure: A New Verse Translation* (Washington, D.C.: University Press of America, 1983).

26 The poem thus bears some comparison with Chrétien's *Erec,* about which Peter Haidu says, "the story of the hero's adventures on a quest for his lady is doubled by the quest of the text for its own generic identity" ("Narrativity and Language in Some XIIth Century Romances" in Haidu, ed., *YFS* 51 [1974]: 135).

27 All Middle English passages from *Sir Gawain and the Green Knight,* and the associated translations, are taken from Volume 2 of *The Pearl Poems: An Omnibus Edition,* ed. William Vantuono (New York: Garland, 1984) and are cited in the text by line number.

28 "Magical Narratives: Romance as Genre," *New Literary History* 7 (1975): 139.

Arthur Coming Alive Again: 18th-Century Medievalism and the Beginnings of a Modern Myth

By KURT GAMERSCHLAG, *Universität Bonn*

☩

Looking at British 18th-century Arthurian pieces from our post-Tennysonian point of view they appear to us today as strange as they would to a medieval reader. This is but the natural consequence of their belonging to contexts of entirely different historical quality not only diachronically speaking but also, as with most cultural concepts, on the synchronic level. From this it follows that we must be aware that what looks like a monolithic conceptual block from a distance will break up into very diversified elements barely interconnected when viewed at a closer range. In other words, what may appear as (and is frequently called) a "medieval movement" or even "revolution," identifiable by a set of unifying principles, becomes such a thing only in the eye of the much later beholder. In reality there was a great multitude of images, prejudices, rhetorical positions, aesthetic concepts and ideological stances with regard to the "Middle Age(s)" in the 18th century. To begin with, for most 18th-century people the term Middle Ages meant a period different from our own reckoning: it is one of the amusing historical ironies that the 16th-century humanists who had first sought to distance themselves as "moderns" from the "medium aevum," in 18th-century periodization became part of that age themselves. We would certainly not do that to the 18th century in our turn today; the example should make us aware, though, that our ideas of the Middle Ages are quite different from those in the age of a Fielding, Walpole, Gibbon, Hume or Bishop Percy.

The total make-up of what is loosely called "medievalism" consists of a vast corpus of material in the arts, architecture, music, philosophy and theology, equal in importance to documents of a literary character. For an attempt at historical re-construction of the revival of Arthurianism as an expression of the wider movement of medievalism the focus on four seminal and interconnected segments out of the total complex of ideas and images may prove enlightening: historiography, popular literature, scholarly literature, and literature with high aesthetic pretensions.

II

Throughout the 18th century historiography was honoured as the most serious and highest occupation of a man of letters. Considering its methods one may distinguish two basic approaches, both with quite venerable traditions behind them: first, the "pragmatic" school of history thinking of its subject – as Bolingbroke phrased it – as "philosophy teaching by examples."[1] Its fundamental assumption was that human nature was unchangeable and ever swayed by the same motivations: in Hume's terms, self-interest on the one hand, and communal interest on the other. Secondly, there was the "antiquarian" school, by most "proper" historians not considered a legitimate part of their profession at all. Often ridiculed for their lack of general vision and their speculativeness the antiquaries concentrated on collecting and conserving the small details of history. Frequently unsystematic but fervent collectors of curious "antiquities" their ranks were filled with amateurs from the clergy and landed gentry as well as professional scholars. As far as the latter were concerned it has been maintained that the period between 1660 and 1730 was one of the highpoints of study with regard to the Middle Ages.[2] A look at the publications of these two generations shows indeed an astonishing output of dictionaries and grammars of the older stages of the European vernacular languages as well as numerous collections of state papers and historical documents of all sorts, including reprints of the medieval chronicles.

As the century wore on these two approaches ceased more and more to be viewed as mutually exclusive by British historiographers. Instead, following the French lead, one turned slowly to consider them as complementary. By mid-century one begins to find attempts at dealing with the wealth of details about customs, manners, social structure and ideas in "Histories of England" that would originally never have deigned to look beneath the level of the great actions of kings and statesmen. As far as the Middle Ages were concerned these cultural explanations and introductions centered on the two fields most strange to the 18th-century Englishman, feudalism and chivalry – the former associated with tyranny and serfdom, the latter with a ridiculous mode of behaviour and expression popularized in the period's aged bestsellers, the neo-chevaleresque romances. Unfortunately for the appreciation of the Middle Ages, however, the historians of the 18th century with few exceptions, only known to very few readers indeed, saw their main business not in understanding the more distant past but in coming to grips with the history of their own modern days and explaining the causes and consequences of the recent great changes in the 17th century. The Elizabethan era was the earliest to be given more extensive notice; everything beyond that was considered exotic and more or less "dark".

If we look quickly at children's histories and other abridgements written for the education of the future leaders of society, like Goldsmith's *Letters from a Nobelman* (1764) or Robinson's *Easy Grammar of History* (1741) we find what the average educated person was really likely to know about the Middle Ages. Here we become aware that the great change towards 'historicism" was still a thing of the future as far as general knowledge was concerned. Nowhere do we see attempts at an outline of crucial cultural, social, or political concepts and structures. Instead, history was treated as in the old pragmatic days as a line of eminent figures or "worthies", while the concentration on modern times led to viewing everything before the Glorious Revolution of 1688 as some sort of pre-figuration. The pre-conquest period got especially short shrift with generally only 3 "worthies": King Alfred, Caractacus / Caradoc, and Boadicea / Bonduca. In very few cases these were joined by King Arthur, cautiously termed "fabulous."

The principle of selection of the historical "worthies" is normally quite explicit: as the present state of government and society presents the apex of development in which the ideals of a balance of power and freedom as well as of polite civilisation have finally been reached the worthies mark the way to this state of perfection. Alfred is, of course, the first law-maker; Caractacus, Boadicea and Arthur share in the role of fighters for British freedom against usurpation, tyranny, and invasion by foreign powers. Arthur, where he appears, is occasionally offset by the weak King Vortigern, who invited the Saxons under Hengist to come to Britain. If we look for the sources from which such historiography would have taken the picture of Arthur we shall have to look to Gildas, Nennius, Bede and Geoffrey, not to the later romances or even Malory.

III

A second field of interest comprises those works of imaginative literature that at least on the surface pretended to deal with the Middle Ages and were thought of as representing some sort of image of bygone times.

As hinted above the popular neo-chevaleresque romances made up probably the largest body of such material. The genre had been formed in the early 17th century as an amalgamation of late medieval material like the metrical romances, Malory's *Morte*, and historical legends and folk tales. The Italian "romantic epics" were another source; a further one was provided by legends of classical antiquity, often filtered through French and Italian channels. The end-product consisted of volume upon volume of complicated love adventures of knights, ladies and damsels in books frequently bearing pseudo-antique titles like *The Grand Cyrus* (1649-53), *Cassandra* (1667) or *Pandion and Amphigenia*

(1665). Their gallant actions, lofty reveries of grandeur, beauty, and happiness were what went by the name of "chivalry" for 18th-century readers – mostly female and of the "leisured classes", as has been frequently pointed out.[3] The genre was still going strong in the 18th century with titles like *The Prince of Salerno* in the 1770's. The late-18th-century debate about the novel and romance in general and the historical novel in particular rang with echoes of this genre as one of the chief enemies to a historical conception of the Middle Ages. *Don Quixote* and the numerous Don-Quixotiads of the same age fought bravely against the neo-chevaleresque absurdities as well.

It was certainly no help in this fight that together with the heroic neo-chevaleresque romances better things were passed on, such as Sidney's *Arcadia* and, especially, Spenser's masterpiece, *The Fairie Queene*. As far as their representations of what was taken for the Middle Ages were concerned, they were not a whit better than the heroic romances. They rather shared with them a fundamentally a-historical approach to their subjects which they tended to develop in symbolical movements of allegorical figures towards unchanging moral truths. Other literary genres of the 17th and 18th centuries, such as the drama and most of the poetry, had this exemplary rather than historical approach, too. It took the development of a new sense of time and space as mechanically measurable and physically present to generate a new look at reality,[4] present and past – and, incidentally, to prepare the ground for a new genre like the novel.

"Chivalry", then, and with it the Middle Ages, had thus acquired quite a bad name among readers of sense. One can understand why Hurd and Percy had to move very cautiously when they tried to prove that the concept and the original literature propagating chivalry made actually a lot of sense and had little to do with the neo-chevaleresque love-and-honour games, the fairies, giants and pompous speechifying. Of course, elements of "real" chivalry as a code of behaviour had survived the dawn of the modern age and had been unconsciously absorbed into contemporary manners: in the language in which a gentleman addressed a woman; or wrote poetry or love letters to his mistress; or challenged another gentleman to a duel; or toasted the king – to say nothing of the code of conduct that was observed by the small professional armies and navies of the time.[5]

In literature outside the romances, whether of the heroic type or written in imitation of Spenser or the Italian master Ariost, the Middle Ages lived on – even if perhaps unconsciously – not in a particular genre but rather in figures. Carried over from Elizabethan and even earlier days, and revived vigorously in the 18th-century, historical dramas made readers and theatre-goers familiar with knights, barons, squires and yeomen. Poetry readers, of course, knew the *Penseroso* and hermit, later added to by priest-&-poet figures like the druid, the minstrel, and the bard.[6] The gothic novel, from the mid-century onward, further supplied nuns, monks and pilgrims, often joined to the traditional enemies of British virtue: the cruel Saxons and Danes, the Saracens and the Giants. Last but not least, one should not forget the famous medieval heroes of ballads and chapbooks, Robin Hood and his band.

Of all figures the 'errant knight' was easily the most popular figure to be instantly adapted by "medievalizing" authors, the new Arthurians among them. He could obviously serve both as a butt for ridicule and as a serious model for imitation. As well-known examples for the ridiculous one could name the numerous Don-Quixotiads of the century or the Gothic-novel parodies. The drama had similar "dis-mantled" heroes in the tradition of *The Knight of the Burning Pestle*. One need only think of Henry Fielding's *Tragedy of Tragedies* (1731) with its debunking of an Arthurian court whose strongest support is the little knight Tom Thumb. The ballads of Tom Thumb from which Fielding took his cue were, of course, a very popular way of making fun of Arthur and his knights, little as was known about the things that were made fun of.[7] In poetry, finally, Chaucer's "Sir Thopas"-tradition was carried on with superb pieces like Alan Ramsay's *Christ's Kirk on the Green* at the one end of the century and John H. Frere's *The Monks and the Giants* at the other.

Against such pictures of knights as braggardish cowards and quarrelsome layabouts in the *miles gloriosus* tradition, of single combat and jousting as drunken brawls, and of courtly love as lecherous peeping and skirt-chasing, the age had to set quite noble images. Most of them go back to Spenser's Prince Arthur and Britomart, such as the Knight of Arms and Industry in James Thompson's famous *Castle of Indolence* (1748). Many knights walk about in heavy Miltonic religious and patriotic armour, like Sir Richard Blackmore's numerous knights – among them *Prince Arthur* and later *King Arthur* of 1695 and 1697. The strongest images in the related line of the knight as *miles christianus*, and as a symbol of virtue battling with the powers of evil, before the turn of the century came from John Bunyan's Christian in the immensely popular *The Pilgrim's Progress* (1678), and from Emmanuel in *The Holy War* (1682). Another popular hero who fought the serpent not only as the symbol of the general enemy to mankind but, at the same time, as the image of the powers that threatened England in particular was St. George, renowned in ballad and song, and readily available for the political rhetoric of the Georges on the British throne. The popular broadsides were furthermore ringing with the praises of more secular knights, like Sir Bevis of Hampton or Guy of Warwick.

Lastly, there were the knights, barons, and attendant figures in the emerging new genre of the Gothic Novel, cast variously in the roles of villains and abductors, or of rescuers and noble heroes. Instead of an airy medieval paradise filled with over-courteous lords and ladies one here finds gloom, barbaric massacre, and religious fanaticism. To the 18th-century reader, however, these evils were obviously and predictably conquerable by knights and "champions of virtue" with values of decency recognizable as one's own.

It is evident that, underlying this, there is no conception of the "gothic" world as different in specific time, as something that is a recognizable past to one's present. We move rather in a world of moral, aesthetic and civilizational values where the label "gothic" is put by different people on different things at different times.[8] Chinoiserie in textiles or in furniture, the baroque style in architecture, the metaphysical manner in poetry, scholastic thinking in philosophy and theology, as well as a whole era of civilization as close in time but distant in spirit as the Elizabethan age, the label "Gothic" covered something that was put up in opposition to the prevailing modern taste. In general, this was a post-Restoration form of the older classicist movement whose earlier phases began to come under attack as degenerate as easily as the uncivilized Elisabethans and earlier periods in the name of new ideals variously defined as "naturalness," "simplicity," "directness" and "sincerity." As frequently happens the new ideals were said to be the old and original ones lost under a welter of aberrations committed throughout postclassical times. Restoration of lost purity became the order of the day, notably in a "neo-classic" revival in architecture and the arts but also in literary writing.

Efforts to infuse the pure and simple spirit took various roads. Some sought the "fundamental" qualities in exotic (pseudo-) Persian or Japanese works supposed to be unsullied by degenerate western culture; others stayed nearer home. They replaced the journey into oriental space with a journey back in time. What they found was "northern", "druidic" or simply "medieval" material to which they ascribed the desired "classical", i.e. fundamental, qualities. Addison's laudation (of a late and corrupt version) of the ballad of "Chevy Chase" is the most famous example for such findings in a search aimed at pre-conceived generalities rather than at specifics. Historic time and physical space obviously did not serve as relevant concepts. Given this attitude it is small wonder that many authors worked with exotic, classical, as well as medieval materials, often mixing forms and styles.

IV

Towards the end of the century more and more frequently polemical rhetoric opposed antiquity and the classicist modes of expression against what were supposed to be medieval principles in aesthetics, poetics, or outlook on life in general. Grossly overstated as most of these polemics may seem today, as the years went by one can see them getting more and more informed both about classical times and about the middle ages in all kinds of details of culture, politics, "manners" and literature.

At roughly the same pace, authors with literary ambitions were getting better informed, too. No sharp distinction between works based on antiquarian research and those written without any greater notion of the traditions encapsuled in the material may be drawn in the early stages of this development, though. Everything is rather a matter of degree. At the lowest point a bare name like Arthur or Merlin would appear in a narrative or a poetic reverie that at best had faint echoes of the Saxon wars, or, at worst, used the names just as eponyms for "good king" and "wizard". At the other end of the scale, some of the traditional story-lines of the chronicles and Geoffrey or of the romances and Malory are discernible, together with the appropriate "dramatis personae" and attempts at recreating an "authentic" background of manners, beliefs, and rituals. The picture is further complicated by the fact that various old traditions, half-starts and genuinely new beginnings came together at this period to form quite a wide spectrum of Arthuriana even at the start of the King's revival.

Among the old traditions one may single out the popular chapbook ballads and stories as well as the Italian and Spenserian refashionings of the 15th to 17th centuries clearly discernible as the background of Dryden and his adapters, as in the much later John Thelwall or J.H. Frere. Other writers, like William Hilton in his drama *Arthur* (1759), made obvious use of older chronicle traditions, although one should, perhaps, be wary of the sources from which the Arthurian elements in names and story-lines could have been gleaned. A reading of Geoffrey of Monmouth may, of course, be possible; just as likely later chronicles, plus information picked up from works like Whitaker's *History of Manchester* (1771) or from Jeremy Collier's revised edition of Moreri's *Grand Dictionaire historique* (1701-1705), may have formed the background.

A third group of writers may best be called "antiquarian". The professors Thomas Gray and Thomas Warton first spring to mind as workers both in the field of imaginative writing and of scholarly research. But there are, of course, lesser known, now even completely forgotten ones: Richard Hole with his epic romance *Arthur: or, the Northern Enchantment* (1789) may be cited here, Caesar Morgan with his poems about the "Shrine of King Arthur" and the "Cave of Merlin" (1783), or even the Shakespeare-forger, W.H. Ireland, with his pseudo-Elizabethan *Vortigern* of 1796, to be immediately countered by A. Portal's *Vortimer*.

It is very difficult, in this context, to appreciate the first phase of the Arthurian and medieval revival without a full consideration of some pioneer groundwork – not the least of which came from Thomas Warton and other "professionals" like Hearne, Thyrwitt, Ritson and the Swiss scholar Mallet. But there were also antiquarian amateurs in the field without whose popularist approach little may have moved. The clergymen Percy and Hurd, later distinguished as bishops, just after the mid-century wrote the texts that from a latter-day's perspective changed the situation or, at least, indicated a basic change in attitude: *Letters on Chivalry and Romance* (1762) and *The Reliques of Ancient English Poetry* (1765).

One of the most significant results of all of these antiquarian efforts was that the popular vision of Arthur as one of the line of "British Worthies" fighting for liberty against invaders and traitors at home, was added to by other and more complex versions. Although Malory had last been reprinted in 1634, not to find another editor till 1815, and although it took considerable energy to trace and get access to medieval romance literature, authors like Warton, Gray, Hole and Thelwall knew more than the *Legendary History of Britain*, first translated into English at the beginning of the century. In fact, Gray and Warton, both intensely interested in literary history, had quite an astounding knowledge of medieval literature, extending beyond Old and Middle English to Icelandic, Welsh and Old French. Hilton, Hole and Thelwall knew at least enough of characters like Mordred, Guinever, Gawain, Lancelot and Tristram, to work them into configurations that made some sense of their old symbolical value. And even if John Seally addressed his opera *The Marriage of Sir Gawaine* to those readers of the *European Magazine* of 1782 "Who Love Antiquity for Its Nonsense More than for Its Sense", he based his work on the findings of Thomas Percy. In general, it is probably safe to say that, through the work of the early antiquaries and scholars, general medieval as well as Arthurian material was not only being made available in a constantly growing and diversified quantity but also slowly but surely was changing its quality. Beginning with a reliance on very recent literary texts or secondary accounts and summaries there was a movement backwards: first to pre-Elizabethan romance, then to older ballad literature, to the re-discovery of Malory and, lastly, to the appreciation of Middle English texts as well as Old French and Middle High German parallel material. All this was supported by the new development in historiography shifting its emphasis towards an understanding of the minutiae of distant cultures and away from looking for "worthies" on and off battlefields.

V

Collecting 18th-century Arthuriana is beset with the problem that an Arthurian name – especially Merlin – might not mean anything closely related to the body of Arthurian stories but could simply belong to the body of popular figures whose names have become more or less synonymous with their special powers or quality. The wizard Merlin appeared in quite a number of popular pantomimes (partly adapted from Dryden's and Purcell's *King Arthur*, partly perhaps going back to Rowley's Jacobean *Birth of Merlin*) that stage him as the proverbial (comic) mountebank or prophet.9 Acting out slapstick harlequinades or functioning as the mouth-piece for after-the-fact prophecies (Swift provided a superb example in his *Famous Prediction of Merlin, the British wizard, Written About a Thousand Years Ago, and Relating* to the Year 1709), Merlin became a generic name associated with almanachs – a fate from which he was not rescued before the turn of the century.

King Arthur fared only marginally better than Merlin when 18th-century chapbook and ballad writers used his name. "Good King Arthur's" pretensions to a noble court and heroic deeds along with most of the chivalric literary tradition were metamorphosed into absurd images and plots that made sense only in ballads like "Tom Thumb", in children's stories à la "Jack-the-Giant-Killer", or in comic operas, burlesques, pantomimes, and parodies.

There are, indeed, two strong traditions of comic Arthurian works in this century – one stemming from Fielding's *Tragedy of Tragedies* (1731) and its devastating attack on the bombastic style and the idealized worlds of the contemporary heroic drama; the other originating in exactly such a drama, the famous *King Arthur* (1691), written by John Dryden and set to music by Henry Purcell. Forgotten today, "burlettas" such as O'Hara's *Tom Thumb* (1780) or an *Entertainment, Call'd, Merlin: or the Devil of Stone-Henge* (1734) proved at least as popular as their serious counterparts.

While the comic pieces turned Merlin gradually into the proverbial pantomime wizard (in an interesting sideline in *Merlin in Love* of 1759 the Merlin-and-Vivien story was adapted to a harlequinade with Merlin as Harlequin's elderly rival for the love of Columbine),[10] and while Arthur was degenerating into the half-witted Atty, Dryden's and Purcell's heroic Arthur not only generated quite a number of serious and comic adaptations throughout the century, but also remained on stage in its own right. In his preface Dryden maintained that he had consulted Bede and other sources for authenticity's sake. In fact, his drama is, for long stretches, a good example of the non-antiquarian approach. It runs on the conventional heroic-drama model, with one plot line developing the grand themes of liberty and honour, and the other balancing this with a private love theme. There are faint echoes of the Vortigern story in the lofty plot line which centers on Arthur's conquest of the Saxon king Oswald. The love plot and many set pieces, from the abduction of the blind heroine Emmeline to an enchanted grove and an omnipresent fairy machinery of spirits and goblins, rings strongly with echoes of Ariost, Tasso, and Spenser. Many later Arthurians, like Scott in his *Bridal of Triermain* (1813), or Bulwer-Lytton in his own *King Arthur* (1825) were fascinated by this latter "romantic" line popular also with 18th-century fairy tale writers.

Apart from these features there is, however, a notable "modern" antiquarian element in Dryden's *King Arthur* in the presence of "northern" or "runic" lore.

We have here the first example of such knowledge as consciously employed in Arthurian literature. One wonders what may have moved Dryden to use this material of nordic gods and rituals: maybe it was little more than a modish response to the beginning "northern" discoveries that were also evident in Sir William Temple's writings of the day (e.g. "On the Death Song of Ragnar Lodbrook").[11] "Antiquarian" poets, from Thomas Gray far beyond Macpherson, have certainly followed this lead, often confusing Celtic / Gaelic and Nordic / Germanic, and mixing them further with chivalry and its attendant themes of feudalism, minstrelsy, and balladry.

It is curious to see two counteractive but sometimes also mutually beneficial movements at work. On the one hand, scholarly research into the literature and culture of the middle ages: Henri Mallet's famous *Introduction a l'Histoire de Dannemarce* (1755), translated by Percy, is one example; Percy's own volumes of *Reliques* (1765) or Warton's *History of English Poetry* (1774-81) may serve as others, that in spite of gentilizing touch-ups kept differentiating and carefully separating the material into "correct" systems.[12] On the other hand, many poets and dramatists insisted on mixing the elements, throwing together classicist, baroque, oriental, "romantic" Italian / Spenserian or "Gothic" materials and styles. Richard Hole's *Arthur; or, the Northern Enchantment* (1789) may serve as just one example. Contemporary reviewers and even modern critics have praised Hole's learning in the Scandinavian and Celtic mythologies pervading a plot which centers on Arthur's battles against the Saxon invaders. The careful mythological distinctions are, however, only one layer. Rhetorically Hole's work is positively Augustan / Vergilian, whereas structurally, his "poetical romance" in seven books imitates the Italian romances mixed with numerous classical epic set pieces, chivalric episodes and well-known devices such as the abducted heroine (here called Imogen, Merlin's daughter).

In his *Fairy of the Lake* (1801), John Thelwall topped this with a fanciful mixture of everything even remotely connected with Arthurian themes. His ground work is provided by a daring telescoping act which puts Nennius' Hengist-and-Rowena story into the days of the Table Round. No Morgan-le-Fay is needed as his Rowena has all the powers of a sorceress over northern spirits plus an incubus. Guinevere is Vortigern's daughter, incestuously desired by her father but in love with Arthur. The plot is too complicated to repeat here; suffice it to say that against the evil Rowena the Lady of the Lake (with attendant fairies) plots for Arthur and his union with Guinevere, in order to bring his valour together with her "Beauty, Truth, and Innocence" in a "Feast of Reason! feast of Sense!"

Set pieces from the Italian romances and Spenser are everywhere, but Thelwall's great success, in an otherwise nearly unreadable closet drama, is Tristan: in a series of superbly comic prose scenes breaking the jogging blank verse Tristan appears as a hard-drinking and rather dim-witted braggadoccio in the Falstaff tradition, punning on heroics from Alexander-the-Great to Jack-the-Giant-Killer, on the strange situation of a mostly empty round table or on the odd behaviour of the gods in Valhalla. King Arthur, too, sometimes looks suspiciously more like Prince Hal than like the champion of virtue and love he is supposed to be in the serious parts of the drama.

Against such fanciful, eclectic pickings from all fields of Arthurian tradition Thomas Warton's sonnets "On King Arthur's Round Table at Winchester" and "Written at Stonehenge" as well as his ode "The Grave of King Arthur" (all pub. in 1777) are very sober pieces indeed. Instead of rashly assuming – as the learned Gray had done in his Arthurian allusions in "The Bard" (1757) – that his public was familiar with the Arthurian background, Warton carefully chose place associations and explained them rather than alluding to and presupposing special knowledge. The Round Table, Stonehenge, Glastonbury, Avalon, Tintagel or Camlan thus could be made to serve his favourite theme of a compromise between pride in the (violent) national past and, at the same time, in the civilized present which could sublimate and celebrate this past in art and ancient monuments.

Some version of this profoundly conservative balancing act between the past and the present, the wild and the ruled, the natural and the polite, is at the root of nearly all Arthurian works of the 18th century. Perhaps one may even suppose that it was the condition from which 18th-century medievalism in general, whether of Warton's learned kind, of Walpole's "gothic" manner, or Hole's and Thelwall's extravagant mixtures, mainly sprung. For all the endeavour to understand the dark ages, the historians remained interested in them only as the preliminary stages of a might-ruled society developing towards the present rule of right.[13] The preoccupation of 18th-century Arthurians with the old problems of royal legitimacy and usurpation, the constant warnings against civil war and internal chaos, as well as the complementary harpings on the nationalist theme of a common, noble history unbroken from Arthur to the present day, underline this contemporary concern with the emergence and keeping of order very clearly. Over and over again, the evolution of British Liberty is seen at the heart of that history, with liberty defined in lofty political terms of being free from occupation or usurpation. Only in comic pieces like Fielding's *Tragedy*, in Thelwall's Tristan, or in some ballads does one sense a definition of freedom in private terms like being able to criticize the pomp and circumstance of the mighty, or to draw attention to the gaps between rhetoric and reality. Praising rather than doubting, defending rather than attacking the *status quo*, agreed with the mentalities of authors whose positions as clergymen, professors, or members of the landed gentry far away from the center of political influence and action, can hardly lead one to expect anything else. For all their professed yearnings for the wild and natural, most were like Warton, Percy, or Hurd embedded in their polite and gentlemanly society which had a place for the unruly things only in art.

And even there the myth of Arthur was a mild and toothless one. It knew of happy reunions after abductions, not of irreparable conflicts; it treated of fairies and sirens happily overcome, not of internal flaws in the "system"; it celebrated final victories over brutal invaders and knew not of the self-destroying bewilderment and the battle in the West. The 19th century was to change this harmless picture of the rediscovered Arthurian world. For one, Malory, re-edited after nearly 200 years, changed many perceptions. Imperial ambitions and disasters, as well as a growing concern with the predicament of the individual in a far-from-faultless society, coloured many others. 18th-century Arthur had begun defending his own island of Britain, asserting his royal right to reign and marry the fair Emmeline – 19th-century Arthur would be quite unsure about his realm and right, and he would marry a Guinevere.

Notes

[1] *Letters on the Study and Use of History* (1735), letter II. Quoted from J.W. Thompson, *A History of Historical Writing*. New York, 1942, II 94 f.

[2] Cf. D.C. Douglas, *English Scholars*. London, 1939, 16 f.

[3] Cf. J.M.S. Tompkins, *The Popular Novel in England, 1770-1800*.London, 1932, 206 ff.

[4] Cf. E. Cassirer, "Raum und Zeit" in: *Das Erkenntnisproblem in der Philosophie und Wissenschaft der neueren Zeit*. Berlin, 1922-23, II, 339-374.

[5] M. Girouard, *The Return to Camelot: Chivalry and the English Gentleman*. New Haven, 1981, 17.

[6] Cf. J.M.S. Tompkins, "In Yonder Grave a Druid Lies," in: *RES* 22 (1946), 1-16.

[7] Cf. K. Gamerschlag, "Tom Thumb und König Arthur; oder: Der Däumling als Maßstab der Welt. Beobachtungen zu 350 Jahren gemeinsamer Geschichte," in: *Anglia* 101 (1983), 361-91.

[8] For the following cf. J. Haslag, *"Gothic" im 17. und 18. Jahrhundert*. Köln, 1963; L. Whitney, *Primitivism and the Idea of Progress in English Popular Literature of the 18th Century*. Baltimore, 1934; M.H. Abrams, *The Mirror and the Lamp*. Oxford, 1953; H. Honour, *Neoclassicism*. Harmondsworth, 1968: M. Butler, *Romantics, Rebels & Reactionaries*. Oxford, 1981.

[9] Cf. L. Gottesman, "The Arthurian Romance in English Opera and Pantomime, 1660-1800," *Restoration and 18th-Century Theatre Research* 8, no. 2 (1969), 47-53.

[10] *Ibid.*, 51. The author of this "pantomime-opera" was Aaron Hill.

[11] Cf. W.P. Ker, "The Literarary Influence of the Middle Ages," in: *CHEL*, Cambridge, 1913, X, 221 ff.

[12] Cf. L. Dennis, "Thomas Percy, Antiquary vs. Man of Taste," *PMLA* 57 (1942), 140-54; J. Butt, *The Mid-Eighteenth Century*. *OHEL*. Oxford, 1979, VIII, 102 f.; J. Pittock, *The Ascendancy of Taste*. London, 1973.

[13] Cf. H.T. Dickinson, *Liberty and Property: Political Ideology in 18th-Century Britain.* London, 1977, 14 ff.

My Search for Morgaine Le Fay

By MARION ZIMMER BRADLEY

✠

The first thing I had to do, before writing a novel on the subject of Morgaine le Fay, was to determine whether she was an actual – as opposed to a legendary – character. Before doing this, I had to find out if there was any truth whatever to the whole mass of Arthurian legend. Some archaeologists – notably Geoffrey Ashe – have spent a lifetime proving it; this should be good enough for a novel, which after all is not a scholarly paper, and deals with invented characters.

Any search for a real-life Arthur, going as it does to the darkest part of the Dark Ages – the very time in English history for which we have no documented evidence at all – must of necessity rely very heavily upon all kinds of other evidence. The first piece that came to my attention was the evidence of names. We may at once dismiss the kind of "evidence" used by such films as *Excalibur,* showing knights in 15th century plate armour; we *know* who was king then. Nor is there any doubt about the succession after the 8th century; the roster of the Saxon kings of what is now England, though perhaps not on the lips of every schoolchild – as is probably the case with the Kings of England after the Norman Conquest – is easily accessible to even such desultory scholarship as mine.

However there *is* a hiatus – a convenient hiatus – after the withdrawal of the Roman Legions and their emperors in the fourth century, and the first of the Saxon chronicles in the Sixth. There, if anywhere, we will find traces of Arthur.

We come first to the name. In Roman Britain, the name Arthur was unknown; when we come to the sixth century, as we see from a few church records, suddenly all sorts of baby boys were being christened "Arthur." This constitutes a hint; people do not name their sons after someone they do not like and admire. (How many baby boys named Adolph are found in England, or for that matter in Europe, in the wake of World War Two? It is likely that this name will not regain its popularity in this century.) Jacqueline was not a common name for girls until Mrs. Kennedy put a *Jackie* into every first grade classroom.

Once we have established that someone named Arthur was at least enough admired for boys to be named after him some time in the sixth century, let us examine what small written evidence there is. The monk Gildas, writing in the sixth century, was lambasting current peoples with not being the fighters – or the patriots – they were in the Good Old Days of King Arthur. There is a monument in Cornwall somewhere commemorating a burial place for Mark, and Drustan; somewhere in my researches I read a reference saying that this stone, mentioning as it does a possible King Mark and Tristan, was the only actual written reference we had to any one of Arthur's knights; but this reference is chiseled in stone; I have seen it with my own eyes in Cornwall. Elsewhere, the monk Nennius – however reliable this eighth century monk may or may not have been – gives us a list of battles; in one of which he says that "Arthur and Mordred" were both killed. It says nothing about the relationship, or lack of same, between them; everything is legend, and for all we know to the contrary, they could have been, not the king and his nemesis, but the dearest of friends. But it we give Nennius any credibility at all, they did exist; and they died.

After Nennius, we come to Geoffrey of Monmouth; and while he was reliable enough for Shakespeare to take from him some plots of so-called historicals, I personally believe he was England's first writer of fiction. Despite his detailed biographies of Merlin and Arthur, I personally would not – alone – give Geoffrey of Monmouth enough credence to hang a yellow dog, or even to write a novel on his say-so; but the evidence of Geoffrey of Monmouth, *with* the evidence of archaeologist Leslie Alcock, points in that direction.

In the very depths of the Dark Ages, then, we find the old Stone Age hill-fort of Cadbury Castle, in Somerset, which, when excavated, shows evidence that *some-one* – whether Arthur or another – re-fortified this defensible place, and occupied it. If he was not Arthur, he seems to have done what Arthur is said to have done; and what was that? Well, between the withdrawal of Rome and the first of the Saxon Kings, Arthur or another, some great chief, seems to have fought a series of battles (at one of which "Arthur and Mordred" were killed) which brought a quarter century of peace to England. This may not seem like much, but there have not been 25 consecutive years of peace in *my* lifetime.

At least this era of peace permitted the Saxons to become somewhat civilized before taking over. So if this Somerset chieftain was not Arthur – and since he left no marks we have found, and probably could neither read nor write, and could not tell us his name – we may as well assume that he was named Arthur, for he seems admirable enough, in those days, for people to have named their sons after him – we will never know.

So for the sake of a novel, if not of a scholarly paper, the evidence is good enough; it was good enough for an archaeologist.

But after finding out to my own satisfaction that Arthur had existed, I found at least four "legendary" family trees for him.

These mostly contained the familiar figures of Morgaine, Morgause, Igraine, etc.; and they also contained, everywhere in the legends, the figure of the Lady of the Lake.

Now, Malory (the main source for these legends retold) does not approve of Morgaine le Fay, making her Arthur's worst enemy and nemesis to the whole world of chivalry. When a man repeats this without citing any evidence for the *evil* of these or any particular women – or set of women – we may assume a religious or cultural bias. We do know that since Roman days, a fierce patriarchy had come into the country with the Norman Kings, and they had many political reasons for that. From reading the works of Tacitus and others, we know that the Celts did not assume a wholly patriarchal culture; this was a matter of religion. This puts us on the track of the Druids.

Now admittedly, we know nothing of the Druids; going to the writings of Julius Caesar and similar sources to find out about the Druids is a little like going to *Mein Kampf* for the fine points of Jewish culture; for most Romans were trying to eradicate what little remained of the traces of such cultures. But by these and other evidences we do know that the Celts were matriarchal, although reports of their matriarchy are probably overdone (and of course we cannot rely on such writings about "Druids" as were commonplace among Celtic Twilight romantic writers), we may say they were not as fiercely patriarchal as the Romans, or the Norman kings who admired them. (Very few peoples were.) To make a common analogy between the Celts and the Eastern forest Indians of North America, the tribes when at home and at peace seem to have been led by women; women at least know more of domestic matters than men, and when a tribe was not at war, in the absence of the fierce Roman-Norman patriarchy, there seems no reason that women should not be tribal rulers; we know it was often done among the Saxons and others.

We do know one thing; in time of war, as we know from accounts of such things as Boadicea's rebellion, the woman who ruled a tribe – the Queen, whatever she may have been called – chose one of her tribe for Duke of War; and one of the things we do "know" about Arthur is that he is called in all the tales *dux bellorum,* Duke of War. Is it too much to think that Arthur may have been chosen one of these Dukes of War? We do know from Roman writings that the Romans had some trouble with the concept that a Queen was not necessarily the property of a king. That there were "Client Queens" we do know from contemporary Roman writings. We also know that the Romans did not approve of them.

We may also assume that it was for some such reason as this that Malory did not approve of Morgaine and the Lady of the Lake; but how do we know they may have existed? Simple; for the reason that, although these women never *do* anything in the stories, Malory could not imagine telling tales of Arthur without them. In other words, they were so much a part of the Arthurian legends that their absence could not be imagined. One wonders how important these women had been before fifteen hundred years of woman-hating clergy got their hands on them.

It does not – at least to me – take much thought to figure out a connection between Lancelot of the Lake and the Lady of the Lake. That there was a lake, we do know; all over Somerset; we find archaeological and other traces that this part of Somerset was under water, part of a great brackish inland sea which was not entirely drained until the Dutch gave help and advice on doing so in the 15th century. In Glastonbury in Somerset – which retains the old name of the Summer Country because only in dry Summer was it dry enough for pasturing cattle – there is a museum showing ancient houses, built on piles in the Lake, by the Beaker Folk, those elusive people – Magdalenians – who reportedly built Stonehenge. (Despite Victorian romance, Stonehenge was built before the Druids ever came to England.)

As for Lancelot, it takes very little thought to define him as a late addition to the myth; he seems to have come from "the French book" for which Malory blames his tale. (If the basis of Arthur's tragedy, as all the legends seems to reiterate, was a King betrayed by his closest friend, we may relegate the role of Lancelot to Bedivere. This is fairly easy to understand; Queen Eleanor of Aquitaine had invented chivalry, and Malory wrote his tale for a romanticized court which had little to do except play games of chivalrous love. He had to invent Lancelot "of the Lake" to add some love interest for that court. And along with Lancelot came Guinevere.

It is fairly easy, then, to create in imagination the rest of the cast of characters. We remark of the Lady of the Lake that at times she behaves like Arthur's best of friends, giving him his sword Excalibur. She must then have been a person of some importance, able to bestow a sword, which again gives us the track of the Druids. At other times, she appears as Arthur's enemy; Morgaine is often referred to as Arthur's enemy, one of the "damsels of the Lady of the Lake" which again suggests a religious bias; yet it is to Morgaine, despite their quarrels, that Arthur appeals at the end of his life.

This elusive matter of Druidism brings me to the wise man Merlin. In living memory in the Gaelic-speaking part of Scotland, the local pastor was referred to, by a simple man, as a "wise Druid." Yet Merlin, in Malory's book (which is admittedly a collection and cannot be looked to for consistency), behaves so inconsistently that in Arthur's long reign that title, (like the Lady of the Lake) or name, may have been held by more than one person; hence the two Merlins in my book.

Speaking of that era, Henry II, one of the greatest of Norman Kings, was what we would now call an Arthurian buff; he liked playing Arthurian games, and liked to think himself a sort of new Arthur. Looking, perhaps, for a kingly grant, the abbot of Glastonbury in the heyday of that place discovered on the grounds – or said he did – the body of a Saxon Chieftain whom he identified with King Arthur and of a golden-haired lady whom he called – what else? – after the French, Guinevere; this may be very well the old Welsh Gwenhwyfar. Some traditions give Arthur three wives, *all* named Gwenhwyfar. Granted there were fewer given names in those days, but this is ridiculous.

The bodies of chieftain and "Guinevere" seem to have vanished – if they ever existed – in the debacle that brought down the monasteries in the days of another Henry, the VIII. It was a rough time, but even so, a body seems a little large – and solemn – to be casually mislaid.

Anyhow, this is enough evidence for a novel. As I say, the chain of evidence, being little more than an inspired series of guesses, would not suit for a scholarly paper; but then I was not writing a scholarly paper. Heaven forbid! I have no talent for that sort of thing.

But it made a pretty good novel.

The Knight Errant: The Quest for Integrity

By RICHARD CAVENDISH

✠

Ladies and gentlemen,

We have come quite a long way together since yesterday afternoon, haven't we? Perhaps you may remember that almost at the beginning of the seminar, the point was made that one piece of evidence for the vitality of the Arthurian legend is simply the fact that the speakers at this seminar come from such a wide variety of disciplines. The phrase used was: we have philologists, historians, and so forth. You have heard from the philologists, and you have heard from the historians – and the so forth is me!

We have heard at our seminar about the real man round whom this enormous body of legends, or really mythologies, as Graham Caie said, grew up. And we have heard about interesting aspects of the romances about King Arthur and his knights in French and in medieval English, we have heard about the revival in the 18th century, and we have heard from a distinguished author of our own time, who has used elements of the legends to create a much-admired novel. What I would like to do is try and round the seminar off by asking a simple question.

You have these stories about King Arthur and you can consider all kinds of things: where do they come from, how did they develop, how did bits of them shift from one author to another, and so on. However, the question I always want to ask is: what are the stories actually about? What do they really mean? I suggest that certain recurring themes keep coming up over and over again, and it is, I suggest to you, in the area of these recurring themes that the answer is to be found as to why the Arthurian legend has retained its vitality.

Stories do actually have meanings. Everything said in words – or words that aren't gibberish (and in the case of James Joyce, even words that *are* gibberish) – has a meaning of some sort. Or rather, it may be truer to say, not that a story always has a meaning resident inside it, like a mouse lurking in a hole, but that meaning can be found in the story, and certainly readers and audiences do find meanings in them. Indeed, they will judge a story and its importance to them very much in the light of what they take its meaning to be. You will have heard the New Testament referred to as 'the greatest story ever told', which by no means is meant to imply that the events related in it did not actually happen. Far from it. What it is meant to imply is that great truths are told in great stories. And I think that is a truthful implication.

It is here, in this question of what the stories of the knights mean, I suspect, that the fundamental reason for the vitality of the Arthurian legends may be found. At first sight this is strange. The stories, after all, are about almost entirely ficitious characters, who did not actually do the things attributed to them in the tales; they are set in a world of make-believe, full of magic and mystery; in so far as they occupy any real world at all, it is the world of medieval Europe, which is light years remote from anything we know today. And yet these old tales still pack a most powerful punch, still impress people as "great stories", with an implication that, though fictitious, they nevertheless are about reality – and are saying something important about reality.

Why have they remained so alive? Well, first of all, I suggest because they are exciting stories. They are full of adventurous brushes with appalling perils, hairsbreadth escapes and apparently inescapable predicaments, beautiful women and brave men, combat and love and death.

Consider, just as one brief example from many, a story about Sir Palomides, the Saracen – the fact that he was an Arab and a Muslim, incidentally, does not seem to have bothered the other knights in the slightest. Sir Palomides went to the Red City, to avenge its king, who had been treacherously murdered by two wicked brothers, named Helius and Helake. After an exchange of taunts and appropriate ruderies, the two brothers rode against Palomides full tilt. The redoubtable Saracen disposed of Helake in very short order, striking Helake through his shield and his armour into his chest and killing him. The other brother, however, Helius, hurled Palomides off his horse with his spear and rode over him. Palomides jumped up and seized his opponent's horse by the bridle and pulled down both horse and man. The two then fought on foot, lashing at each other with their swords, and Palomides was outmatched. He grew weary and faint, and Helius drove him about the field.

"Then," Malory says, "when they of the city saw Sir Palomides in this case they wept and cried and made great dole, and the other party made as great joy."

"Alas," said the men of the city, "that this noble knight should thus be slain for our king's sake."

"And as they were thus weeping and crying, Sir Palomides, which had suffered an hundred strokes, and wonder it was that he stood on his feet, so at the last Sir Palomides looked about him as he might weakly unto the common people how they wept for him, and then he said to himself, "Ah, fie for shame, Sir Palomides. Why hang you your head so low?" And therewith he bore up his shield and looked Sir Helius in the vizor and smote him a great stroke upon the helm and after that another and another, and then he smote Sir Helius with such a might that he felled him to the earth grovelling. And then he raced off his helm from his head and so smote off his head from the body.

And then were the people of the city the merriest people that might be. So they brought him to his lodging with great solemnity, and there all the people became his men."

You must grant that that is exciting stuff!

Second, and more importantly, the Arthurian stories impress us because they enshrine and they uphold certain values – values which people everywhere in the world admire, and it seems always have admired: loyalty, courage, generosity, courtesy, honourable conduct, straightforwardness, gentleness to the weak, truthfulnes, reluctance to take unfair advantage. The values of the gentleman. The values of the chivalrous knight.

"By my head," says Sir Lancelot of somebody in the *Morte Darthur,* "he is a noble knight and a mighty man ... and if he were assayed, I would deem he were good enough for any knight that beareth the life. And he is gentle, courteous and right bounteous, meek and mild, and in him is no manner of mal engin, but plain, faithful and true."

And later on in the book Lancelot himself is made the subject of what must be one of the noblest eulogies ever composed. After he has died, his body is taken to Joyous Garde, his castle, and is lying in the coffin. His brother Sir Ector comes in and stands by the coffin and looks down at him:

> "Ah, Lancelot," he said, "thou were head of all Christian knights. And now I dare say," said Sir Ector, "thou Sir Lancelot, there thou liest, that thou were never matched of earthly knight's hand. And thou were the courteousest knight that ever bore shield. And thou were the truest friend to thy lover that ever bestrode horse, and thou were the truest lover, of a sinful man, that ever loved woman, and thou were the kindest man that ever struck with sword. And thou were the goodliest person that ever came among press of knights, and thou was the meekest man and the gentlest that ever ate in hall among ladies, and thou were the sternest knight to thy mortal foe that ever put spear in the rest."

There were, of course, real knights errant in the Middle Ages – William Marshal being a celebrated and redoubtable example. What a real knight errant did was to travel round fighting in tournaments to make money, not unlike a present-day professional boxing champion. An Arthurian knight errant, though, is a different animal, and quite uninterested in money.

It is significant, isn't it, that the Arthurian legends have such an important place in the ancestry of the modern thriller, adventure story and Western? – the type of story in which the hero goes out into the world to risk his life for his ideal of what he ought to be, and to right wrongs – wrongs which the forces of society, officialdom and the law do not right. As in Raymond Chandler, 'down these mean streets a man must go'. As in many a Western movie, a stranger rides into town where an evil of some kind has established itself. He puts an end to the evil by main force, by fighting and killing somebody – and then he rides on his lonely way again.

It is a theme which has come into considerable prominence again in very recent years, sometimes in a disquieting way, as the law, the police and the courts seem so often powerless or even disinclined to protect ordinary citizens against attack. The hero takes the law into his own hands, because the law does not work or is corrupt. In this same way the Arthurian knight errant rides out from headquarters in Camelot to help the oppressed and unfortunate, put right injustices and generally make the world a better place.

Take, as one of innumerable examples, the episode of the Castle of Evil Adventure in *Yvain* by Chrétien de Troyes. The hero, Yvain, who is a knight of the Round Table, one evening comes to a town and heads towards the castle, where he hopes for hospitality for the night. The people of the town shout rudely at him, telling him that if he stays there, he will be sorry. They do not explain why. Nor does a polite elderly lady, who explains to Yvain that the apparently surly townspeople are only trying to save him from doing something he will regret. Now, of course, to tell a knight of the Round Table that he had better not risk encountering some frightful unspecified peril is only to make absolutely certain that will rush off at once to confront it. He could not live with what his fellow knights would think of him, or with what he would think of himself, if he dodged the danger.

So Yvain goes on into the castle, where he finds a kind of sweatshop, in which 300 ragged, half-starved girls are toiling over embroidery. It turns out that they come from the Isle of Maidens, whose king sends a tribute of 300 girls to the castle every year. Many a good knight before Yvain has tried to rescue them and failed. The custom of the castle is that any knight who stays there must fight single-handed against two exceptionally formidable warriors, who are the sons of a demon by a human woman. Yvain stays the night and the next morning he goes into combat against the two demonic brothers and kills them both. Then he sets the captive girls free and ends the tribute.

Although the knight errant does much good in the world in this way, it does not appear that this is really his central purpose. The good he does seems to be a by-product of his knight errantry (and the same point can be made, I believe, about Raymond Chandler's hero and the hero of many a Western). What the knight errant is doing, it seems, is testing himself. He is testing his skill as a fighter, his courage, his readiness to cope with every situation that he meets and with any odds, however steep – to triumph over every difficulty, every discouragement, every danger. He lives by incessantly stretching his nerve and measuring himself against odds.

And that explains why the Arthurian heroes in the main are not what you would expect them to be, if they had been brought up in the English public-school system! They are *nervous*, they burst into tears not infrequently. If they are turned down by some girl they go mad. I have lost track of how many times Sir Lancelot goes mad because things go wrong for him with ladies. They stretch their nerves, and so they are nervous. They are not – at least most of them – brutish heroes. A point I want to come back to shortly. Now, why is the knight errant doing this testing himself, this stretching himself all the time?

One of the principal reasons he does this is to gain renown. He lives in a world where reputation is enormously important, and when he does something heroic he is likely to take quite a lot of trouble to make sure that news of his exploit is carried back to court, to win the admiration of the other knights and the fair ladies. One of the key ingredients in the concept of honour – of being an honourable man – is that of being honoured, being a man of respect (shades of *The Godfather*!), who is respected himself and pays a decent respect to others.

Another reason for knight errantry, quite often anyway, is to win the love of a lady. The knight needs to show himself worthy of her, and his passion for her lends strength to his arm in combat. But what seems to matter to him even more than her love is the fact that she inspires him to heroic exploits – and it is these exploits that he apparently values for their own sake. One of the constantly recurring themes in the stories is the conflict between love and action, with the love of a woman as the force which keeps the hero away from the world of action and so threatens to dishonour him. Over and over again, a fay or an enchantress, drawn to a knight by his heroic vitality, lures him to her bower, her enchanted island, her paradise garden where it is spring all year round and the flowers are always in bloom and the trees ever in blossom – where there is no time, in other words, and no change. But this will not do for the hero. He becomes restless and dissatisfied. He needs the world of time and change, because he needs to develop.

There seems consequently to be something deeper that the knight errant is searching for. I suggest that it is his true and best self or himself raised to his highest power, as you might say – a perfect integrity of character forged under the hammer blows of combat and danger.

It is crucial that the hero is a *fighting* man, for very often in real life the professional fighting man – the career soldier or sailor or airman – is not in that occupation because he is a bloodthirsty brute. On the contrary, he may well be a surprisingly gentle, peaceful sort of person – away from the field of battle, at least. He is a professional fighting man because it is only in fighting that he is able to operate fully on all cylinders, only then that all his best qualities of courage, intelligent grasp of a complicated situation, power of rapid decision, power of command, all move into high gear at the same time. Only then, in a fight, is he most fully his best self. That is why he likes fighting.

And that point is brilliantly made by Lord Tennyson – incomparably the greatest writer to retell these stories since Malory – in some lines he has about Arthur himself:

> "When Arthur reach'd a field of battle bright
> With pitch'd pavilions of his foe, the world
> Was all so clear about him that he saw
> The smallest rock far on the faintest hill,
> And even in high day the morning star."

You do not need to read many biographies of Lord Nelson, for example, to see that he was a man of that kind. On land he was really rather inadequate. You remember that celebrated occasion when the great Duke of Wellington met him and was profoundly unimpressed by what seemed to him at first to be a silly, vapid, conceited person. But put Nelson on the deck of a ship, and then put him anywhere within the remotest possible reach of a battle – even if it was miles upon miles away – and he would crowd on all sails and fret and dance about with impatience on his quarterdeck and make the most frenzied efforts to get himself to the scene of action. Not because he was a brute who loved killing: on the contrary, he was loved for his gentleness. But because he was only his truest, his most complete and best self in a fight.

This surely is what many medieval career fighting men – knights – were like in real life, and this is surely what the Arthurian knights are like. The point is brought out in a reverse way by the only character in the Arthurian legends who, I thought until yesterday, has a sense of humour, Sir Dinadan. The great advantage of cowardice, he remarks at one point is that it keeps a man alive – a most unArthurian comment.

Dinadan is the friend and companion of Tristan, or Tristram, whose appetite for fighting is absolutely insatiable. At one point Tristram asks Dinadan help him attack thirty opponents at once, and though Dinadan very sensibly says that to fight against such odds is patently ridiculous, Tristram drags him ruthlessly into it. Later on, a bruised and weary Tristram and Dinadan arrive at a castle, where by a typical Arthurian custom, they can only obtain hospitality for the night by defeating the castle's champions. "Oh well," Dinadan says, "in that case let's go somewhere else for the night." But of course Tristram will not hear of that. So they fight the castle's champions and vanquish them, and then they are just settling down comfortably for the night when two of their fellow knights of the Round Table, Gaheris and Palomides the Saracen, arrive outside, wanting a place to spend the night. This is fine with Dinadan, who would be perfectly happy to let them in, and welcome, but no, no, Tristram says that he and Dinadan are honour bound to keep up the custom of the castle by challenging Gaheris and Palomides to fight. Dinadan grumbles, but it does him no good. He is badly bruised in jousting against Palomides, stops fighting, says he has never in his life met anyone madder than Tristram – except possibly Lancelot – and rides away in a huff.

Dinadan is a subversive character because he does not share the knightly ideal of attaining integrity through struggle and conflict. The other characters in the stories are puzzled by him and regard him as a jester and a cynic. I always wonder what medieval audiences made of him.

There are hints here and there in some of the tales that the hero who achieves integrity, achieves in some way a triumph over death –death which he has repeatedly risked in the course of his adventures.

A good example of a story that brings some of these threads together is the tale of the Fair Unknown, as told by Renaud de Beaujeu.

The hero is Guinglain and he is the son of Gawain by a fay, but at the beginning of the story he does not know who his father is or who he is. This is strikingly driven home by the fact that he does not know his own name – the simplest and most fundamental mark of identity. He is brought up by his mother alone and she calls him Fair Son.

Eventually, the story says, Guinglain went to Arthur's court and asked the king to grant him whatever he asked. Arthur agreed and decided to call him the Fair Unknown, because he was strikingly handsome and strangely anonymous. Suddenly another stranger arrived, a girl named Hélie, escorted by a dwarf. She asked Arthur to send a knight with her to rescue her mistress, Blonde Esmerée, Queen of Wales, who had been turned into a dragon by two enchanters. She could be released from the enchantment only by a kiss. Guinglain at once volunteered and Arthur, bound by his promise, had no alternative but to send him with Hélie. She was not at all pleased to be given a young, untried, unheard-of knight as a champion. She rode away in a rage and Guinglain had to hurry to catch up with her.

However, as they rode on their journey together, Hélie's attitude to the Fair Unknown began to change, as he showed himself a brave and resourceful champion against the dangers on the way, overcoming various redoubtable knights and giants. Presently he and Hélie came to the Golden Island, where a knight defended the causeway across to the island against all comers. His efficiency was indicated by a row of helmeted heads impaled on spikes. Guinglain challenged him, fought him and killed him.

On the island was a palace with crystal walls and seven black towers and a garden of trees and spices where the flowers bloomed and the birds sang all year round. The lady of the island was the Maiden of the White Hands (La Pucelle auxs Blanches Mains) a fay of matchless loveliness, as radiant as the moon gliding out from behind a cloud in the night sky. Unknown to Guinglain, the Maiden had long been in love with him, and now she announced her intention of marrying him. Guinglain was strongly attracted to her, but Hélie reminded him of the mission he had undertaken to rescue Blonde Esmerée, the queen turned into a dragon. So next morning he and Hélie stole away from the island.

Presently they came to the Waste City of Senaudon, where poor Blonde Esmerée was immured. They reached the city in the evening. Once a fine city, it was now in ruins and apparently abandoned. Guinglain rode in alone through the broken gate, past crumbling towers and through deserted streets to a vast marble palace. At each window of the palace stood a minstrel, with a lighted candle, playing and singing. The minstrels called a welcome, but Guinglain cursed them. He rode into the hall and halted by a massive table. A knight came from a dark room and attacked him, Guinglain driving him back, but then being assailed by axes, wielded by no visible hands. Then a huge knight rode against him on a fire-breathing horse. Guinglain stood his ground and killed the knight, whose body turned into a mass of corruption in front of him.

Then the minstrels left, slamming the windows shut and taking their candles with them. Guinglain now waited in the darkness and felt horribly afraid. A glow of light spread through the hall. It came from the eyes of a hideous firebreathing serpent, which glided towards Guinglain and kissed him full on the mouth. He heard a mysterious voice saying that his name was Guinglain and he was the son of Gawain. Overjoyed and completely exhausted, he feel asleep on the table.

When he woke up the hall was full of light and by his side was a beautiful woman, though not quite as lovely as the Maiden of the White Hands. This was Blonde Esmerée, the dragon restored to her human form by the kiss. She told Guinglain that the two enchanters, Mabon and Evrain, had bewitched her and driven the people of the city away. Mabon was the knight on the fire-breathing horse killed by Guinglain the night before. Now she intended to marry Guinglain.

Guinglain agreed but his heart was with the Maiden on her island, and later he went back there and he and the fay consummated their love. But when news came that Arthur had determined to hold an important tournament, the fay knew that she could hold Guinglain with her no longer. That night he went to sleep in her arms, but when he woke up he was in a wood with his horse and his armour beside him. He acquitted himself nobly at the tournament and was reunited with Blonde Esmerée. They went to Senaudon, where the people of the city had now returned, and Guinglain and Blonde Esmerée were married and crowned king and queen with tumultuous rejoicing.

At the beginning of this story, Guinglain does not know who he is. The quest is a search for his identity and only by braving its perils and hewing to his duty does he discover his real self. But this is not all. When he frees Blonde Esmerée from the enchantment, he breaks the spell on the city and restores it to life. The sorcerers, Mabon and Evrain, represent the power of death. They kill the city, in effect, driving the inhabitants away and turning it into a ruin. The minstrels, with their corpse-candles and their avid welcome, which must not be returned, are the walking dead. Mabon himself is dead and so his body putrefies instantly when Guinglain defeats him. Guinglain brings the Waste City back to life and 'marries' it by wedding Blonde Esmerée. He becomes its king, a king of life, and the people greet him with rejoicing and acclaim because he has won a victory over death.

He also wins the Maiden of the White Hands by his valour, but it is the human queen he marries in the end, not the beautiful fay in her paradise. It is here that he achieves his full integrity. The fay is a snare. In her way she is another representative of death, and the road to her realm is set with severed heads. The hero's true path lies in this world, not in the delectable otherworld with its ravishing garden, where time stands still, and its delectable mistress.

There are many parallels between Renaud de Beaujeu's story and the final episode in Chrétien de Troyes's story of Erec and Enide. Here the hero is besotted with his lovely wife Enide and moons over her and stays in bed with her half the day. When he discovers that people are laughing at him he sets out on a long journey, taking Enide with him, during which they meet and overcome a whole series of perils.

The last adventure on their journey is recounted in the mysterious "Joy of the Court" episode. They come to the town of Brandigan, the stronghold of King Evrain on an island in a deep and rapid river, where there is an enchanted garden. No stranger has ever gone into it and come out alive. Erec is determined to try it, of course. In the beautiful garden, where it is summer all year long and the birds sing sweetly, he sees a row of sharp stakes, each topped by a severed human head. These are the heads of the champions who went there before him. There is one empty stake, waiting ominously for Erec's head, and on it hangs a horn. No one has ever been able to sound this horn, but whoever does will win honour and fame above all other men.

Further into the garden Erec sees a beautiful woman sitting on a silver couch in the shade of a tree. Her lover, a gigantic knight in red armour, appears and challenges Erec. They fight savagely until the red knight, exhausted, at last yields to Erec. His name is Mabonagrain. It is he who killed the previous champions and he has been held captive in the garden by his beautiful mistress until a knight comes and defeats him. He has fought his best, but is only too glad to have been beaten and he will be set free when Erec sounds the horn. Erec takes the horn and sounds it loud and long. Mabonagrain is freed, and

King Evrain and all the townsfolk are beside themselves with joy – the "Joy of the Court".

After this Erec goes back to Arthur's court and succeeds his father as King of East Wales. Arthur gives Erec and Enide a magnificent coronation ceremony.

Mabonagrain's bondage to his mistress in the garden parallels Erec's earlier besottedness with Enide, and Erec sets him free of it. But this hardly accounts for the supreme honour which Erec wins in the adventure and the delicious rejoicing with which his success is hailed. Here again we have a realm of death, approached past rows of severed heads and defended by a warrior in bondage to a beautiful woman. Here again we have a garden where time stands still, and flowers bloom and birds sing all year round. Here again, I suggest, we have a hero winning a triumph over death and here again at the end of the story he is crowned as a king. To be crowned as a king, symbolically, means to be recognised as someone who is raised above the ordinary human level, who has achieved an ideal integrity of character. "Ideal manhood closed in real man": in dedicating the *Idylls of the King* to Queen Victoria, Tennyson said that was what the legends were really about.

The theme of the quest for integrity and so for the conquest of death reaches its culmination in the Grail stories. The Grail is the symbol of, and in the legends somehow the container of, the vivifying power of nature and so of God. Hence its associations with the fertility of the land, with lavish feasting, and at the same time with the Last Supper and the lifegiving, immortality-conferring blood of Christ.

The quest of the Grail can only be achieved by the best knight in the world, which if I am right must mean the knight who most perfectly achieves integrity. If he achieves this, then does he conquer death by becoming immortal? The Grail, after all, is the vessel of the holy blood, which is the wine of the Eucharist. The consumption of the bread and wine of the Eucharist mysteriously united the worshipper, momentarily at least, with Christ, who himself gained the most momentous victory over death of all – the victory which guaranteed for all faithful Christians immortal life in heaven when their time should come.

In the First Continuation to Chrétien's *Conte del Graal* Gawain partly succeeds but partly fails at the Grail castle. He asks about the bleeding lance, which is the one that pierced Christ on the cross, but he is so desperately weary that sleep overwhelms him before he can ask any more questions. He then wakes next morning to find himself alone with his horse in a field by the sea. The evening before the country all around him had been barren and desolate. Now it is all green and streams are flowing. Now there are people about, where there had been none before, and we are told that there would have been more of them if Gawain had only asked more questions. Those who see him riding by call out to him: "Sir, you have both slain us and healed us! Thus you should be glad for one reason and sad for the other – glad because of the weal that we now enjoy, for well we know that you are the cause. Yet we should hate you because you did not learn whom the grail served. No one could tell the great joy that would have come of asking ..."

This 'great joy' recalls the joy of the people of the Waste City, restored to life by Guinglain, and the delirious rejoicing over Erec's success in the adventure of the Joy of the Court. Now both these exploits seem to have been victories over death.

The people tell Gawain that he has healed them but also slain them. If he had stayed awake long enough to ask the crucial question, would he have brought them immortal life?

If Gawain had achieved this, he would have been a second Christ. Later on, in the *Queste del Saint Graal,* the Grail hero, Galahad, is virtually a reincarnation of Christ on earth. The earlier Grail stories seem to have implied that the best knight in the world could attain salvation and immortality for himself and for others, because he was the ideal man – because through his own experience and adventures and the great quest for the Grail he had *become* the ideal man– not through the channels of the Church. This was not a view of spiritual progress that the Church was anxious to encourage.

Well, if you can't beat them, join them. The Grail quest was taken over by Cistercian monks and turned into Christian propaganda. A brand-new Grail hero was invented, Galahad. His mother, Elaine, is the daughter of the Fisher King, so that the hero is of the line of the Grail Keepers. His father is Lancelot, who to any right-thinking person is obviously the best candidate for 'best knight in the world', but who is now systematically disparaged and discredited. In a brilliant stroke of irony, Lancelot makes love to the beautiful Elaine while under a spell which causes him to mistake her for Guinevere, Arthur's queen, the woman he truly loves. So the great knight fathers the pure Grail hero while in his mind and heart committing the sin of adultery which will debar him from winning the Grail himself.

Galahad, by contrast, will be a virgin all his life, which now becomes a crucial qualification for success in the quest. The Cistercian version, indeed, reflecting its monkish origins, is quite obsessed with horror of sexual desire. But furthermore, the earlier idea of the good knight reaching integrity and immortality by his own efforts is now most positively contradicted. The sinfulness of humanity is far too profound for that. Only the grace of God, undeserved and freely given, can bring man to salvation. The whole spirit of the earlier Arthurian romances is undermined. The first three virtues, in order of merit, as listed by one of the *Queste del Saint Graal*'s irritating swarm of hermits are virginity, humility and patience. These are scarcely the virtues of the Arthurian heroes of yore.

Galahad himself is a throughly unsatisfactory character, made of cardboard, who has no failings at all and so he cannot develop, or grow in any way. He does not find his true, ideal self in the quest because he is perfect to begin with. The purpose of the Grail quest is certainly to achieve immortality, and Galahad in the end is taken up into heaven by angels. But his success brings no benefit whatever to his fellow men. Indeed, the Grail is taken away into heaven and never seen again, so that no other hero shall have a chance to aspire to and attain it. It seems a sad and bitter perversion of a noble theme.

Members and Associate Members of the Symposium

Aagot Andersen
Flemming G. Andersen
Hanne Bønløkke Andersen
Ida Anine Andersen
Ole Andersen
Geoffrey Ashe
Irene Ashe
Birgitte Balsløv
Hans Basbøll
Connie Beck
Lise Bek
Helene Bekker-Nielsen
Karen Bekker-Niselsen
Phillip C. Boardman
Marianne Børch
Else Borris
Erik Borris
Marion Zimmer Bradley
Keith Busby
Graham D. Caie
Richard Cavendish
Søren Bo Christensen
Dorrit Einersen
Ann Gamerschlag
Kurt Gamerschlag
J. Gerritsen
Stefanie Gropper
Louis Hjarvard
Paul Horstmann
Per Ingesman
Bodil Heiede Jensen

Kurt Villads Jensen
Jørgen Kampmann
A.M. Kinghorn
Riti Kroesen
Sigurd Kværndrup
Christa Kühnhold
Hanne Lange
Louise Lillie
Vibeke Matorp
Julia McGrew
Morten Nøjgaard
Ivar Orgland
Birte Ovesen
Rita Pedersen
Viggo Hjørnager Pedersen
Thomas Pettitt
Iørn Piø
Mette Pors
Margit Rest-Westmeier
Reinhold Schröder
Lone Søderstrøm
Leif Søndergaard
Bengt Algot Sørensen
Stofnun Árna Magnússonar
Ulrike Strerath-Bolz
Aage Trommer
Henrik Tvarnø
Casper Tybjerg
Elisabeth Vestergaard
Søren Vinterberg
Morten Lund Warmind

Below is the Menu that was served by "Restaurant Amfita" on the evening of November 17th to celebrate our Symposium. We borrowed the recipes from a feast given by Richard II of England and the Duke of Lancaster on the 23rd of September, 1387.

MENU

From the great feast given on September 23rd, 1387, by King Richard the Second and the Duke of Lancaster:

Slete Soppes:
Take white of leeks and slyt hem and do hem to seeth in wyne, oile and salt. Rost brede and lay in dysshes and the sewe above and serve it forth.

Tartlettes:
Take pork ysode and grynde it small with safronn. Medle it with ayren and raisons of coraunce and powdor fort and salt, and make a foile of dowhg and close the fars thereinne. Cast the tartletes in a panne with faire water boillyng and salt. Take of the clene flessh withoute ayren, and boile it in gode broth. Cast thereto powdor-douce and salt, and messe the tartletes in disshes and helde the sewe thereonne.

Connynges in Cyrip:
Take connynges and seeth hem wel in gode broth. Take wyne greke, and do thereto with a porcion of vynegar and floer of canell, hoole clowes, quybibes hoole, and oother gode spices, with raisons, coraunce and gyngyn ypared and ymynced. Take up the conynges and smyte hem on pecys, and cast hem into the siryppe and seeth hem a litel on the fyre and serve it forth.

Crustade Lombarde:
Take gode creme, and levys of Percely, and Eyroun, the yolkys and the whyte, and breke hem ther-to, and strayne thorwe a straynoure tyl it be so styf that it wol bere hym-self. Than take fayre Marwe and Datys y-cutte in ij or iij and Prunes and putte the Datys an the Prunes and Marwe on a fayre Cofynne y-mad of fayre past and put the cofyn on the oven tyl it be a lytel hard. Thanne draw hem out of the oven. Take the lycour and putte ther-on and fylle it uyppe and caste Sugre y-now on, and if it be in lente, let the Eyroun and the Marwe out and thanne serve it forth.

Departing from Odense on the morning of November 18th the lecturers are from left to right:
Professor Phillip Boardman, Richard Cavendish, Dr. Flemming Andersen, Chairman of the Centre for the Study of Vernacular Literature in the Middle Ages, Professor Keith Busby, Geoffrey Ashe, Dr. Graham Caie, Mrs. Ann Gamerschlag, Marion Zimmer Bradley, Mrs. Irene Ashe, Mette Pors, Research Fellow and organizer of the Symposium, Dr. Kurt Gamerschlag.